TRUE STORIES
of Elmira, New York

Volume 3

By James Hare & Diane Janowski

This book is a selection of their freelance articles
in the Elmira *Star-Gazette*

True Stories of Elmira, New York, Volume 3

Copyright © 2018 James Hare & Diane Janowski
Elmira, New York

ISBN: 978-0-9994192-4-3

Printed in the United States of America

First Edition

Cover image: Postcard view of Mayor Daniel Sheehan's residence on Maple Avenue, Elmira, New York. Published by Rubin Brothers, circa 1912.

*Dedicated to those who preserve
Elmira's history....*

Table of Contents

True Stories of Elmira, New York
Volume 3

Elmira's Largest and Leading Dry Goods Store

SHEEHAN, DEAN & CO.

136-138-140-142 WEST WATER STREET

Star-Gazette (Elmira, New York) · Fri, Jun 25, 1909 · Page 4

The Story of Sheehan, Dean and Company

By James Hare

June 16, 1909, was a grand day for Elmira, as Mayor Daniel Sheehan would marry Miss Ellen Loretta O'Herron "in a church setting which in many respects was more beautiful and impressive than any seen in this locality in years." St. Cecilia's Roman Catholic Church, which had been dedicated May 7, 1905, was decorated "from the curbstone to the altar," by the artistic Florist Leavitt who had made the "setting for the brilliant occasion one to be remembered for a lifetime."

The couple would settle into their new home on the south side of the city, recently purchased by the Mayor. The house at 361 Maple Avenue (it is The Christmas House today) had been built in 1894 by the architects Pierce and Bickford. The Queen Anne style reflected a philosophy of wealth and success exemplified by its new owners.

The contrast between that wonderful day and the humble origins of Daniel Sheehan are stark. He was born November 1, 1862, of hardworking Irish immigrants in Bradford County, Pennsylvania. His father was killed accidentally while logging in the woods when Daniel was very young. The family then moved to Elmira. Daniel peddled milk after school, eventually quitting school at age fourteen. He worked on a farm and then began work as an errand boy at Strauss and Samuels Dry Goods store. He made $2.00 a week working from 7AM to 10PM. He was "quick, industrious and dependable." As time progressed he took on more responsibility. In 1883 he went to work for Fish & Holmes Dry Goods Company that was eventually bought out by Dey Brothers in 1888.

At that point Daniel Sheehan organized a business of his own with two partners.

Mayor Daniel Sheehan's Residence, Maple Avenue, Elmira, N. Y.

This beautiful home at 361 Maple Avenue is today's The Christmas House.

Three years prior to Sheehan's birth, on December 2, 1859, Elmer Dean was born in a log cabin, in a thick woods near the town of Spencer, New York. When Elmer was four, a fire seriously damaged the family farm causing the family to pack up and move to Milltown and, for a time, Dean's Corners in the Town of Catlin. At age six Elmer became a wage earner in a woolen mill greasing cotton so it would unite with wool to make thread. The family moved to Elmira in 1868, although Elmer lived with a sister in North Chemung.

According to legend, as reported by George Davis for the *Sunday Telegram*: "It was early Autumn. The snow was flying in the air and a chill wind already was sweeping down from the north... a little boy, barefooted, was plodding along the road behind two farmers. 'Whal,' remarked one of the farmers, 'this kinda looks like we're gonna get one of them Winters like we had in '52 when the snow was so deep we couldn't even go to the barn without snowshoes.' 'Yep,' replied the other... 'sure looks like we was goin' to be snowed in all Winter and not even be able to go to Elmira'...." Elmer had dreams that night, and the next morning gathered his belongings in a package at the end of a stick and returned to his parents at Harper and East Oak Streets in Elmira.

He had a number of jobs, and in 1873 went to work for E. B. Satterlee and Company selling butter, eggs among other goods. When the store closed, he became a salesman, at $6 00 a week. Eventually he went to work for Fish and Holmes where he met Daniel Sheehan. Dean became a buyer for the company.

Sheehan and Dean, along with Daniel Richardson (a former professional baseball player with the New York Giants) became partners in 1888 and opened their own dry goods store. According to the Elmira *Telegram* on September 16, 1888 they made the right decision for the paper announced the opening of a "Dry Goods Palace." The paper noted that, "if years of experience, pluck and energy in unlimited quantities, and friends by the thousands count for anything, the phenomenal trade which Sheehan, Dean and Company have been doing since they opened their magnificent new dry goods store at 124 West Water Street.... will not only continue but will grow in extent and volume." The prediction proved correct as the business grew so rapidly that it relocated in 1894 and in 1907 moved to occupy a new four story building at 136-142 West Water Street.

Sheehan, Dean and Company experienced an evolution in marketing and sales. When they entered the merchandising business there was little advertising of any kind. Business was conducted based on barter and the "methods of booth and bazaar prevailed." The rule was never to let a customer get away without selling something. Buyers and sellers engaged in "verbal fencing bouts." According to Sheehan, had a retail dealer advertised "one price" and practiced no deviation with customers, he would have failed miserably.

In 1875, John Wanamaker, "prince of merchants" in Philadelphia, first advertised "one price, always, forever and your money back if not satisfied." It took a number of years for this "new system" to be introduced in Elmira. Sheehan said, "the prevailing methods in trade are always set by the public." Much of the public thought it a right to bargain.

In 1963, the store closed. Daniel Richardson had died in 1926. Daniel Sheehan retired in 1934, Elmer Dean died in 1940 at age 81. The Sheehan's bought out the Dean interests in that year. The corporate name was changed to Sheehan's Incorporated in 1947. Daniel Sheehan passed away in 1951 at age 90. In 1954 ownership of the company passed to Southern Tier Stores, Inc., and the store moved to State Street.

When a child, Elmer Dean had noticed that when climbing an icy hill, one could not stop in the middle of the hill without losing ground. The lesson he learned, he said, was, "if one stops in his work in his effort to progress, he will surely slip backwards in the direction of failure. To be successful and reach the top of the hill, a man must keep on plodding." Both Daniel Sheehan and Elmer Dean were self-made men who overcame challenging circumstances to become owners of a large business establishment.

An advertisement, celebrating fifty years of business, taken by the employees of the company in the *Star-Gazette* on June 29, 1939 stated, "The History Of Sheehan, Dean and Company Is A Story Of Faith! - Faith In Elmira! Faith In Its People And Faith In A Sound Merchandising Policy."

Elmira in 1828

By Diane Janowski

What was Elmira like in 1828?

The *Star-Gazette's* December 29, 1928 edition was dedicated to Elmira's 100th anniversary. It claimed Elmira in 1828 was a hardy little village on a tract of land bounded by Sullivan Street on the east, Columbia Street on the west, First Street on the north, and Hudson Street on the south. "Downtown" was on River Street (today's Water Street) between Lake and Baldwin Streets. A dense pine forest stood on the site of the Erie Station. The population was 3,029. Our main industries were seven grist mills and ten saw mills. We also manufactured linen and cloth.

That edition said it was not uncommon to still see Native Americans "strolling placidly down River Street." Our stores offered coffee, guns, gunpowder, brown sugar, chocolate, blankets, soap, cloth, candles, whiskey and more. Inns and taverns served nut brown ale that kept locals and visitors happy. Wolves howled in the nearby hills.

In 1828, the Tioga River (later that year it officially became the Chemung River) was narrower and deeper than it is today. It was still the main route of transportation to Waverly and Wilkes-Barre, Pennsylvania. The Chemung Canal had not yet been dug. Rafts and flat-bottomed boats came up the river from the south with goods for stores. A winter flood in 1828 left huge ice blocks five-feet thick "scattered up and down Water Street." It was thought in 1826 that the Chemung River might be navigable by steamboat. An outfit in Wilkes-Barre sent Captain Elgar upriver on the ship Codorus to Elmira. Apparently, the situation did not work out as well as expected, and we never saw Captain Elgar again.

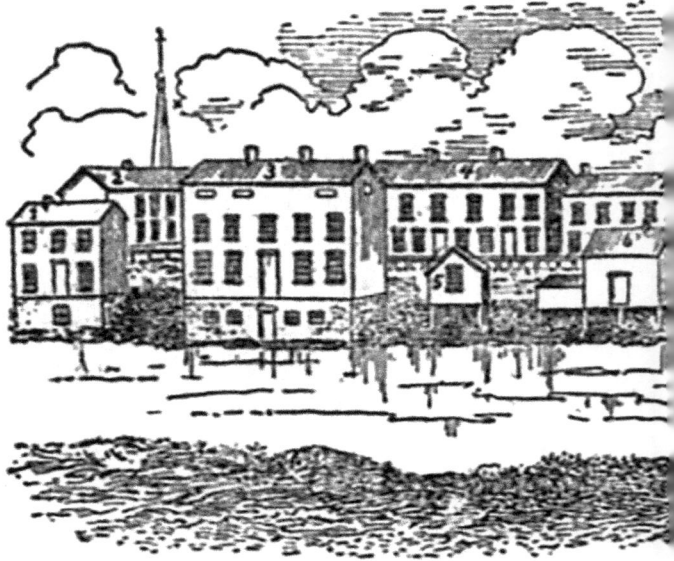

View of the business block of Elmira on Water building may be identified by comparing the numbers in Baldwin Street. 1—Albert Beckwith, merchant. 2—Wid and others. 5—Dr. Mosier. 6—Briggs' Blacksmith Sho 10—Unknown shop. 11—Maxwell & Reynolds; Lawren Court House.

Stage coaches clambered through town on their twice-weekly schedules. The Black Horse tavern on Market Street was Elmira's "hotel stop-over" for the Owego, Elmira, and Bath Stage Coach Company. The "O E & B" was part of a larger system of travel throughout the northeast. From New York City to Angelica, New York the trip was 316 miles and took about 5 days. A few connections could be made north and south along the way. One can imagine the coach and dashing horses. Tavern and inn owners graciously accepted guests. They were dotted along the routes for food and drinks, and overnight accommodations.

There were no banks yet in 1828 and residents didn't use currency, but rather traded or bartered for items they needed. The Chemung Canal bank opened five years later. Its second building on East Water Street now houses

...etween Lake and Baldwin Streets drawn in 1832. The
...ture with those below. X—Presbyterian Church spire on
..., boarding house. 3—Old Masonic Hall, 4—Uriah Smith
...s. Cherry. 8—Postoffice. 9—Aunty Clymer's candy store.
...ers; F. Burrit and the Jones' stores. 12—Dome of the

the Chemung County Historical Society.

Elmira had two newspapers at the time - the *Weekly Whig* and the *Gazette* (also weekly at the time but became a daily in 1856). The Whig only lasted about a year while the *Gazette* continues today as the *Star-Gazette*.

Only a few churches existed. Elmira had one Presbyterian and one Methodist Episcopal church at the time. No fire department protected Elmira. Neighbors and bucket brigades did the best that they could in fighting fires. We had no police department, but a sheriff went from town to town on a regular schedule. One could complain to him if one had a problem.

A covered wooden bridge crossed the Chemung River at Lake

Street. It was built of heavy timbers. It was a toll bridge costing 5¢ each way. A ferry boat crossed at the foot of Conongue Street (today's Madison Avenue.) The ferry boatman lived in a house near the river end of Robinson Street.

Park Church had not yet been built. A narrow path led to Elmira's "little red school in the woods" in the area of today's Wisner Park. It was a school house by day and a meeting place by night.

Not many people today know that the natural course of the east branch of Hoffman Creek meandered the grounds of today's Elmira College, St. Patrick's church, the Hilliard Corporation, and the Clemens Center. It emptied into Newtown Creek near Kennedy Valve. A swamp and a pond stood on the block bounded by West Clinton, Columbia, West Third and Davis Streets. Residents fished for shiners and bullheads. That pond was drained many years ago.

In modern day Elmira it is hard to imagine our city in its early days, but even then there were plans for civic and economic growth, for new businesses, and ideas for attracting new residents. Who knows what the next incarnation of Elmira will look like.

Norman "Chuck Jennings

By James Hare

George Washington, a New York 185-pounder, fought Chuck Jennings, "250-pound Elmira Negro (sic)" in a six round bout at the Kalurah Temple in Binghamton. The fight, "resulted in a win for the Elmiran when he connected with a right to the jaw that sent Washington into dreamland at 2:05 of the fifth round. It was a slam bang battle all the way until Jennings connected with the kayo wallop."

Wally Bader was a heavyweight from Scranton who also fought Jennings. The newspaper reported that early in their bout, "a hefty blow to the body in the first round convinced Bader that Jennings…was an old meanie who played it rough. Wally winced like a rassier during an act of pain and took a nine count."

Al Mallette, the longtime sports reporter and columnist for the *Star-Gazette*, and a good friend of Jennings wrote that, "Chuck Jennings is like the hero of the old west—a peace and quiet guy who'll go out of his way to lend a hand. That is until you raise his dander. Then watch out. You've got to contend with 260-pounds of a man who knows how to use his dukes." That heavyweight boxer and the man Malette described, outlined the philosophy which guided him to found Glove House, "with a little love and kindness you can change a boy's life."

Norman Lorre "Chuck" Jennings was born in Orangeburg, South Carolina on March 30, 1921. Family legend has it that he was a "big" baby. As a child, he was bullied and teased for being "fat." Unlike his siblings he did not pay much attention in school, although he sang

Chuck Jennings in a publicity photo in the Elmira *Advertiser* July 26, 1950 page 7.

and recited poetry. In 1924, the family had moved to Elmira, as Chuck's father was a railroad fireman and work was plentiful here. Eventually folks at the Neighborhood House saw something in Jennings, and asked him to join a boxing class. According to his widow, Nellie, "Walt Bosley, the boxing instructor, saw a big fat kid, who was very light on his feet, a good eye and good balance and very fast." The fat would become muscle and he liked boxing. Nellie noted that boxing was a "character builder" for Chuck physically and emotionally, although his mother did not like him boxing.

Boxing was very popular in the Elmira area from the turn of the 20th century into the early 1950's. Bouts were staged at the old Grotto Park, Majestic Theater, Dunn Field, the Armory and old Eagles Hall. Elmira Hall of Fame boxers were Steve Halaiko, Art Sykes, George (Cyclone) Williams and Jennings.

Halaiko had the longest career. In 1931, he fought Sonny Dorfman before 10,000 fans at Dunn Field. He was listed as one of the Top Ten lightweights from 1929-1934. Art Sykes was a "rugged heavyweight" fighting in the pro ranks from 1933-38. He fought Joe Louis on October 24, 1934, he lost. Eventually he was rated among the Top Ten heavyweight boxers. "Cyclone" Williams fought professionally in the late teens and early 1920's. Former county historian Tom Byrne wrote that, "he always thought he could have been a world champion if he could have gotten the right fights, but in those days, it was hard for black boxers to get bouts that would bring national attention." Williams ran a gym in the old Realty Building and was instrumental in the development of Jennings. Williams was also a minister at the AME Zion Church.

Jennings began boxing at the Neighborhood House at age 12 in 1937. He had 75 amateur bouts over five years, winning the District Golden Gloves heavyweight title in Buffalo and the National Golden Gloves championship in New York City in 1940. In 1942, he turned pro, but then joined the Army. While in uniform he won the all-service championship at a tournament in Manila in the Philippines. Chuck served from March 1943 to February 1946. Upon leaving the Army he resumed his pro boxing career. The boxing circuit was Elmira and Binghamton, New York and Wilkes-Barre and Scranton, Pennsylvania.

A Scranton writer tabbed Jennings as "Old Poke Chops," noting he "is the biggest, perhaps best liked fighter Elmira has produced." He had 200 fights as a pro over ten years, facing Max Baer and Joe Louis in exhibition bouts and beat Jersey Joe Walcott in an army base fight. He returned to Elmira in 1951 and fought his last fight in 1952.

According to Nellie, as his boxing career progressed he became a "party boy." She noted that he became "restless" as he began to look at himself, praying for guidance and started to ask himself what he really wanted. Upon his return to Elmira, he began volunteering at the Neighborhood House. Al Mallette observed that he had been street educated and wrote that Chuck once told him that, "not finishing school was the biggest mistake of my life. I have found over the years that the lack of education is a cross that is terribly heavy to carry...."

At this time he also met Nellie Mae Lewis. They courted and he eventually asked her grandfather for permission to marry her. Her grandfather had two conditions, he said, "we are Methodists and Republicans and I want to carry on that tradition." They were married October 10, 1953, registered Republican and became active at the Frederick Douglas AME Zion Church. They would have one son, Charles Robert, born May 14, 1963. (Chuck would be proud of him today as he is a PhD.)

Chuck had become part of the volunteer staff at the "Nabe." He was meeting youngsters who had no family support, many on their way to trouble. He was also hearing from parents. A vision began to develop about serving these young men. Eventually he was working three full time jobs, raising a family and working to help young people find direction. His hard work, along with the respect he earned from the community would lead to the fulfillment of his vision.

His contribution to the community took many forms. Not only did he actively work with young people, but he also served on boards of many organizations to improve the quality of life in our city. He was Chairman

BOXING FANS
BASEBALL BENEFIT BOXING SHOW
GROTTO PARK
Friday Night, March 15, at 8:30 O'Clock
STEVE HALAIKO
National Lightweight A. A. U. Champion
VS.
JOE LATONA
Buffalo and Niagara District Champion

LEW PROCINO—Cook Academy
Boston A. A. U. Tournament Finalist
VS.
CHARLIE WHITE
Buffalo's Best 160-Pounder
ALSO 7 OTHER WHIRLWIND BOUTS
All Classes
GENERAL ADMISSION $1.25
Reserved Seats at Lagonegro's Cigar Store

Star-Gazette (Elmira, New York) · Tue, Mar 12, 1929 · Page 14

of the Volunteers on Improving Conditions on the Eastside, a member of the Southern Tier Employment Council and the Chemung County Board of Human Relations, as well as serving on the boards of the Volunteers of America and the Chemung County Economic Opportunity Program. The "proudest day of his life" was when Glove House opened. It was his dream come true.

Chuck Jennings died in October 8, 1976 at the age of 55. The Rev. Jay Parker began his eulogy with "Hang in there baby," a favorite Jennings message of encouragement. Art Wellington noted that "Chuck had a knack for communicating in that soft voice of his inner strength to a kid who needed self-confidence and self-discipline. He lived brotherhood every day."

Quoting from Jennings favorite poem, *"Invictus"* Parker read,

"I am the master of my fate, I am the captain of my soul."

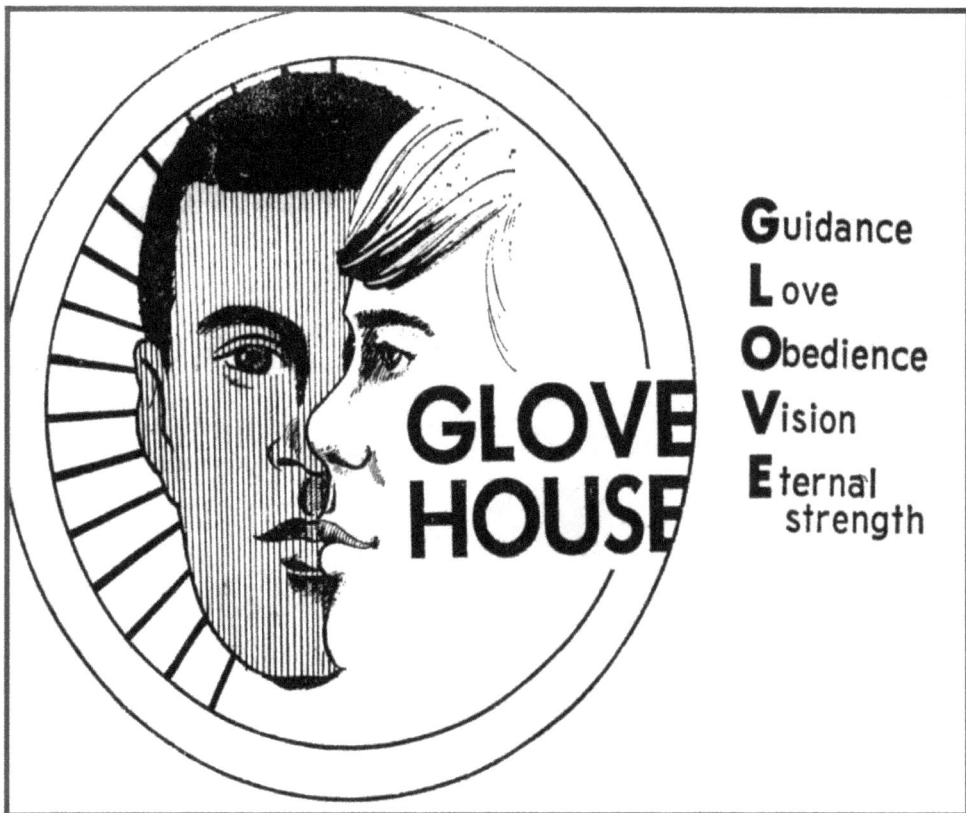

GLOVE HOUSE

Guidance
Love
Obedience
Vision
Eternal strength

Star-Gazette (Elmira, New York) · Sun, Apr 5, 1970· Page 18

Dear old EFA on Lake Street, now the home of Finn Academy. Photograph from the Elmira Free Academy 1923 yearbook *The Archive*.

School Days of 1923

By Diane L. Janowski

The students of Elmira Free Academy, class of 1923, started their final school year on September 1, 1922. "EFA" was then located at today's Finn Academy on Lake Street. As the young men and women walked to school in their brand new clothes from Iszard's department store and shoes from Endicott-Johnson, they hummed the popular tunes of the day. Favorites were "Oogie Oogie Wa Wa;" "Hot Lips;" You Remind Me of My Mother;" "I Wish That I Could Shimmy Like My Sister Kate;" and, of course, the popular "Yes, We Have No Bananas."

New phrases and words were heard in old EFA's halls, like "Yeah," "Scram," "Long time no see," "The cat's whiskers," You're the doctor," and "Nerts." The smart kids were "wisenheimers."

That first week of school was exciting. New teachers and new subjects greeted the young students. Clubs recruited fresh members. Students joined Agora (the girls' debate club), Pep Club, Drama Club, Glee Club, Student Council, and Life Club.

Many of the same students came back that fall: Mildred Gardner, the girl with the reddest hair in class; Edna Ferris, who was in love with silent screen star Richard Dix; Elizabeth "Idgy" Cook, who learned to play the ukulele; Peter Howell, voted the "handsomest boy"; Leon Sanborn, the "heartbreaker" who loved automobiles; Milton Burt, the class president; Ivan Smith, the "most bashful," who played center field for the baseball team and scored two runs in the final game; Madelyn Mack, the "most dramatic," an aspiring actress; Helen Rose, the "most interesting," a member of most clubs; Gertrude Houck, the "best looking," but smart too; Charlotte Bauer, a good jumper on the basketball team; Margaret Wilson, who always loved a good joke and laughed until she cried; and Margaret Mills, "the last girl in Elmira to 'bob' her hair."

Louis Janowsky

Mildred Gardner

Joseph Riley

Leon Sanborn

Gertrude Hauck

Madelyn Mack

Peter Howell   Margaret Mills

Photographs from the Elmira Free Academy 1923 yearbook
The Archive.

School was going well that autumn, but sometimes the pressures of teachers, classes, and homework were just too much and the children needed a safe haven to sit and contemplate the future. That place was the Borst & Cuffney Drug Store on Lake Street, where young minds could enjoy a soda, a dish of ice cream, or hot chocolate after school.

In 1922, there were many after-school activities for students in Elmira. One weekend, Tom Mix and his horse, Tony, were in town promoting their new movie *Just Tony*. At the Strand and Regent theaters, students flocked to see Trimmed starring Hoot Gibson, Scaramouche with Rudolph Valentino, Wild Bill Hickok with William S. Hart, and Rosita with Mary Pickford.

Football games were also important. The 1922 season attendance at EFA games broke all records. On October 7, EFA battled Union-Endicott in a steady downpour of rain that did not dampen the spirit of the filled-to-capacity crowd at Dunn Field. Of course, EFA won.

On October 14, a football parade began at 1:00pm for the "Biggest Game of the Year" against Bingo (Binghamton's nickname). The Bingo cheerleaders arrived early, nattily attired in their white trousers with a big "B" (these were boy cheerleaders). The entire city turned out with such an uproar and enthusiasm it looked like Elmira was celebrating some big college team game. The parade began at Lake and East Clinton Streets. More than 2,000 local students, in addition to the crowd that came over from Bingo, followed a brass band all the way to Dunn Field. All traffic stopped near the parade. Businessmen, lawyers, and persons of every vocation joined the parade. Of course, EFA won, with the winning goal made by Raniero DeFilippo, halfback, who ran 75 yards.

Other contributing team players were Harry Marshall, linesman; Joseph "Red" Riley center; Walter Shafer, end; Leo Bolley, halfback; and Ward "Po Po" Fields, fullback. At the close of the football season, the student council held a banquet in honor of the team.

Dances and parties allowed students to try out a new dance called the "Charleston." School fraternities such as *Lambda Sigma* and *Alpha Zeta* regularly held dances at the Masonic Temple (now Elmira's Hazlett Building) with music by the Peerless Orchestra or the Five Melody Boys. The Senior Reception on December 1 brought 400 students in attendance at the Federation Building.

The dreaded Regents exams took place the week of June 18, 1923. Tests included algebra, geometry, shorthand, English, Spanish, Latin, biology, bookkeeping, geography, history, trigonometry, typewriting, physics, chemistry, economics, French, commercial law and business writing.

The graduation banquet was held June 23, 1923 at the Federation Building. On Monday afternoon, June 25, the graduation list appeared on the wall outside the office. Not every student went home happy that day. On Wednesday, June 27, EFA graduated 178 students, its largest commencement to date. Commencement was held at the school with Mildred Gardner singing the class song and Jean Frasier giving the valedictory speech.

What became of EFA's Class of 1923?

Raniero (Ramon) DeFilippo practiced as an Elmira lawyer; Milton Burt became an insurance agent; Peter Howell was an executive for AT&T and was active in local politics; Leon Sanborn worked for American LaFrance before leaving Elmira; Mildred Gardner was the secretary for the probation office; Ivan Smith became a partner of Frawley & Smith Pocket Billiards of Elmira; Gertrude Houck Vetter and Madelyn Mack Pettit graduated from Elmira College; Charlotte Bauer was a telephone operator; Virginia Carr was a teacher all over the world; Maude Crane was a stenographer for American LaFrance; Elizabeth Cook taught school in Corning; and although he did not graduate with his class, Louis Janowsky married classmate Frances "Pooch" Judson, "most optimistic," and became an engineer for Corning Glass Works.

Commencement Programs To Be Held June 21 and June 22 — Expect 173 Academy Pupils Will Be Graduated.

Star-Gazette (Elmira, New York) · Tue, Jun 5, 1923 · Page 5

START JUNE 20 TO BUILD PLANT

Kennedy Valve Company Building to Go Up With Great Speed.

MAKE CHANGE IN PLANS

Buildings Will Be Built of Brick Instead of Concrete as at First Planned—Company Will Keep as Much of Work in Elmira as Possible—All Up by Fall.

Star-Gazette (Elmira, New York) · Tue, Jun 12, 1906 · Page 7

Kennedy Valve Comes to Elmira

by James Hare

"The future industrial success of Elmira is assured. There is no longer doubt of the fact that "The Queen City of the Southern Tier" is to become one of the most important manufacturing centers of this section of the country... Elmira is to be the future home of the well- known firm, The Kennedy Valve Manufacturing Company, and this city thereby becomes the gainer to the extent of 400 more wage earners."(Elmira *Advertiser*, February 17, 1906).

The decision by Kennedy Valve to locate in Elmira came after a vigorous competition over two years with twenty-one other cities. According to the *Advertiser*, "Elmira was chosen because of its unexcelled natural commercial facilities, among which the great shipping facilities of four trunk line railroads stand out prominently and because there was an active Chamber of Commerce here with a substantial working fund to back up their efforts."

Daniel Kennedy (1849-1928), the founder of the company, emigrated from Ireland in 1866, at the age of seventeen. He settled in New York City. In 1877, he started making valves in a shop on Gold Street in lower Manhattan. The business was immediately successful, eventually occupying four floors of the building. By 1890, the company, needing more room, built a complete new plant in Coxsackie, New York. The business continued to increase, the shipping facilities became inadequate and there was no room for expansion. A new location was needed and Elmira was chosen.

An important issue to be resolved once the decision to locate here was made, was where to locate the plant. Apparently rumors spread that it would be located on the old State Fair grounds near Elmira Heights or above Eldridge Park. On the evening of March 1, 1906, at a meeting in the Hotel Rathbun the question was answered. The company decided to purchase the East Water Street site which had been offered to them. It was reported that the property was owned by Matthias Arnot, "and was originally valued at $1,000 per acre." Arnot sold the plot to Kennedy Valve for $400 per acre and "gave them for $8,000 a property valued at $20,000 and for which he paid $24,000 some years ago." In addition Mr. Arnot had donated $10,000 to the Chamber of Commerce development fund.

On July 11, 1906, ground was broken for the new plant. The company announced that construction of the Elmira plant would be awarded to local contractors. The Elmira *Evening Star* reported on June 22, 1907 that "Power Turned On At The Enormous Plant of The Kennedy Valve Company... It will probably be nearly a month before the first heat is obtained in the foundry, but smoke is rolling from the power house chimney."

Postcard view of Kennedy Valve, published by Baker Brothers, Elmira, NY.

By 1921, the operation had grown to the extent that Kennedy purchased the old Bridge Company plant on East Miller Street, the site of the former Ellis Smith Foundry, (site of F. M. Howell plant today) for a Southside plant. At that point the company employed 1,200 workers.

The Southside plant would close in 1954. The plant produced millions of malleable iron pipe fittings each year. The East Water Street plant manufactured valves and fire hydrants of great variety and sizes.

Daniel Kennedy died on January 14, 1928. His obituary noted that he was, "still president of the corporation in active charge of its policies and management… He was naturally of a retiring disposition… His philanthropies innumerable, but were carried out anonymously…and lived to see many of the sons and even grandsons of old time employees grow up in the business." Kennedy's home at 359 West Church Street was the site of his funeral. At the writing of this article, the home (circa, 1870) is being "stabilized" by Norb Miller Contracting with funds from a grant secured by Historic Elmira Inc., and the Near Westside Neighborhood Association Inc., who is the current owner.

In 1962 the Grinnell Corporation purchased Kennedy Valve. In 1963, Kennedy Valve purchased the Mathews Hydrant from R. D. Wood Manufacturing Company. In 1969, the Grinnell Corporation was purchased by ITT Fluid Technology and Kennedy Valve. Kennedy Valve became a wholly owned subsidiary. In 1988, the current owners, McWane, Inc., of Birmingham, Alabama purchased Kennedy Valve.

The Miller Block and townhouse as it looks today. Photo courtesy of the writer.

South Main Street's Miller Block and Townhouse

By Diane Janowski

In my capacity as Historian of the City of Elmira, New York, one of my greatest pleasures is to assist in the preservation of historic structures. Elmira has remaining, a few significant houses and commercial buildings. I am happy to report that as of this writing, a large and important building on South Main Street is under consideration for placement on the National and New York State Registers of Historic Places. This honor will help preserve the property and will enable the owners to apply for benefits for upkeep and improvements.

I'm talking about the "Miller Block," located at 228-230 South Main Street at the corner of Henry Street. Valentine Miller was a German immigrant and businessman in Elmira for forty-five years. He and his wife, Kate, had ten children. They were early settlers of "Southport." Valentine Miller was a grocer on the Southside and a city councilman. He helped to establish the South Main Street shops. His first store on the northeast corner of South Main and West Henry was remembered for its "excellence and variety."

Valentine Miller raised prize winning short horn cattle, namely "Strawberry Second" and "Strawberry Third" in 1902 and "Elmira Boy" in 1906.

In 1887, Miller hired Architect Huron O. Smith to design and build the Miller Block and Townhouse, directly across the street. In the Italianate style, it is a three-and-a-half story commercial building on South Main and a double townhouse on West Henry connected by a narrow arch. The townhouse is two stories with eight bays and an ornate second story porch.

A prominent stone at the top states "V. Miller Block 1887." The building was designed for use by stores, offices, and meetings. The ground floor was used first as Valentine Miller's grocery, then it passed on to his son Frank Miller.

> ## VALENTINE MILLER.
>
> Valentine Miller, a business man of this city forty-five years, died this morning at 8 o'clock, after an illness of about ten days. He was seventy-six years old and is survived by his widow and ten children, also one brother. Mr. Miller was an active business man and a grocer of the Southside, and was an alderman several terms. He also served as a member of the police commisison several years. The funeral will be held at the family home, 218 West Henry street, Wednesday at 2 p. m. The Rev. Arthur B. Rudd of Grace church will officiate, and burial will be in the family plot in Woodlawn cemetery. Flowers are gratefully declined.

Star-Gazette (Elmira, New York) · Mon, Apr 10, 1911 · Page 7

After a fire in 1913 across the street at the Chemung Grocery store, the owners purchased the Miller property two days after the fire. They moved what was left of their contents into the store and held a "fire sale," including canned goods whose labels had burned off, and all of their smoked meat.

Over the years, all sorts of businesses and organizations used the Miller Block. The top floor was used as a lodge for the International Order of Odd Fellows until 1934. As the housing needs of Elmira escalated, the upper floors were converted into apartments in the 1930's and 40's.

The second floor once held a chiropractor's office and law offices. The third floor was a large open space, big enough for banquets and meetings. Behind the building was a smokehouse and coffee roaster.

In 1950 the first floor was a shoe repair store, and a tobacconist. The

FIRE

SALE

The slightly damaged stock of Chemung Grocery Co. canned goods at your own prices ---labels burnt and smoked contents are unhurt.

223 SOUTH MAIN STREET

New tenants of the Miller Store had a fire sale. Advertisement dated February 7, 1913 in the Elmira *Star-Gazette*.

last alterations to the building were made in 1952 when the storefront windows were updated. Everyone in the present generation should remember the ground floor storefronts as the Panosian family's "Street of Shops."

The application for the official designation and placement on the State and National Registers of Historic Places comes from Michael Lynch, Deputy State Historic Preservation Officer and Director of the Division for Historic Preservation. In his application he writes: "The Miller Block is one of the only remaining architecturally and historically significant buildings along a once vibrant commercial corridor that stretched from Partridge Street to the Chemung River."

"Huron O. Smith's design for the Miller Block was an eclectic mix, rich in decorative features and detail that was far more stylistically expressive than earlier commercial local block buildings. [...] The Miller Block's presence represents this important chapter in Elmira's history of how a building was adapted to meet the needs of new clients and community in general."

Update: The Miller Block was accepted to the National Registry, and restoration of the building is underway in 2018.

Sources:

Elmira *Telegram* April 16, 1911
Elmira *Star-Gazette* January 15, 1913
Elmira *Star-Gazette* February 7, 1913
Application for the State & National Register of Historic Places 2017. Michael Lynch.

SUMMER HOUSE AND ELECTRIC FLOWER BEDS,
RORICK'S GLEN PARK. ELMIRA, N.Y.

Postcard view of Rorick's Glen. Published by Baker Brothers,
Elmira, New York.

Legends of Rorick's Glen

by James Hare

O n June 18, 1900, Elmira's "new pleasure resort, Rorick's Glen Park" opened. The Elmira *Daily Gazette* reported that the audience, "crowded the auditorium to its limit, and this means a good deal as there are easily 1,500 seats which were all filled, to say nothing of many hundreds who were standing or resting comfortably on the grassy hills which form a natural amphitheatre outside the playhouse within good view of the entertainment going on inside." The paper went on to say, "the new theatre was a surprise to the most sanguine. There is certainly nothing its equal in this state in the way of a summer theatre...."

While the theatre opening on June 18, marked the first show of the first season, the park had "opened" to the public on "Decoration Day" at the end of May. The *Daily Gazette* noted, "the Maple Avenue Railroad Company is back of the plan to make this garden spot of the city beautiful and a refreshing place for Elmirans and visitors to rest and keep cool during the hot afternoons and evenings in the coming summer season... After 9:30 o'clock in the morning we have shade and at no time during the day after that is there sun shining in the park... All patrons of the Maple Avenue Railroad are to be given the free privileges of the park. Those who go on their own wheels will have to pay five cents admission."

The history of Rorick's Glen is one of legend, and a story of business, theatre and recreation. The stream flowing through the glen forming pools and miniature falls has been compared to Watkins Glen and Montour Falls, but on a smaller scale. A legend explains its origins. According to the account printed in the May 25, 1911 edition of the Elmira *Star-Gazette*:

> "In the years before Columbus... an Indian maiden, good to look upon dwelt in her father's deer-skin tent on a hill where now runs Ror-

ick's creek. Her name, Chi-we-nah, signifying beauty, was known to all the young men of the tribe and one in particular, Min-to-wan, did the maiden regard as one she might love; but love does not always find a response where it is sent, and alas for Chi-we-nah the young man wooed and won another. Thereafter the hapless maiden laughed no more—then finding a rocky ledge near her father's home, wept there such copious tears that in time, so successive and continuous her grief, presently furrows began to appear in the hillside and where her tears fell, a spring burst forth, and, as if in sympathy, has continued to signalize her grief; and as her grief at last wore her life away, so the stream carved itself deeper and deeper and thus appeared the vast gorge known in later times as Rorick's Glen."

Native American history and legend form the foundation of the story of the glen. The "Indian Steps" were a conspicuous feature of the glen. Legend has it that the Indians cut the steps in the rocky ledges of the "abrupt" river side in order that from their canoes as they landed on the shady shore they could more easily reach the hill-top solitude and among the trees hold their council fires and deliberations free from disturbance. According to author Claude Westbrook, for many years the location was known as, "the Indian Council Chamber of the North."

A story related to the Council Fires is that of a Seneca Chief, who had a beautiful daughter, "recognized as the most famous beauty of the northeast," who fell in love with a Mohawk chief, who returned her love. When the Seneca chief learned of the romance, he forbade his daughter from meeting her lover and placed her under guard. Forbidden his love, the Mohawk chief climbed the cliff above the steps, waved to his lover, and threw himself into the river.

Some hold to the story that General Sullivan's march through the valley "on his errand of destruction" frightened the Native Americans so that they fled up the steps and remained there until his army had passed on up the valley, and then made their way back into Pennsylvania.

Indian Earth Works at Roricks Glen, Elmira, N.Y.

Postcard view from Rorick's Glen. Published by Baker Brothers, Elmira, NY.

ELMIRA, N. Y. NEW BRIDGE AT RORICK'S GLEN.

Postcard view of Rorick's Glen and bridge. Publisher C.S. Woolworth, Elmira. Collection of Diane Janowski.

In a story about the "pioneer days along the Chemung," we learn of the massacre of Aholiab Brown and his family on July 4, 1779 at the mouth of Rorick's Glen. Brown had left Wyoming County in Pennsylvania to settle on the banks of the Cowanesque. Having navigated the Chemung River, through hostile Seneca territory, he established himself. But his wife Mercy was struck by disease and required care, so he had to abandon all and return to his former home.

At the glen, he saw a vast assemblage of warriors who had been attending their usual July pow-wow. Brown attempted to quietly and secretly pass them by. But the "savages" were aware of his presence and the attack began. They approached his boat with stealth, covering their canoes with boughs of branches. Knowing that surrender meant torture Aholiab took out his musket. "Many a dusky foe tasted the waters of the Chemung before they reached his boat. However they came in numbers so large Brown, his wife Mercy and two others were tomahawked and thrown in the river and the boat was set on fire." A party of former soldiers of Sullivan's army, who had settled in the valley, discovered the attack and went to the rescue, but in vain.

The *Star-Gazette* reported on July 2, 1907 that, "this realistic incident of pioneer life on the Chemung in early days will be reproduced with all the vividness lent by the latest addition of electrical effects previous to the canoe parade at Rorick's Glen (the scene of the real incident) on the evening of July 4 immediately after the performance of the Manhattan Opera Company."

The first use of the glen was for lumbering and it was during 1848 that it was acquired by those who gave it their name.

To paraphrase the late Paul Harvey, the rest of the story is in the next article.

ELMIRA, N. Y. Roricks Glen Theatre.

Postcard view of Rorick's Glen Theatre. Published by C.S. Woolworth & Co., Elmira New York

Rorick's Glen Park

By James Hare

"**B**efore the days of the auto, the movie and the dance craze, it was an honest-to-goodness fact that Elmirans in summer had two places to go, "Rorick's and home." So many preferred Rorick's that the familiar slogan "All cars go to Rorick's" finally became literally true.

Attending the Rorick's opera was as much a duty as breakfast, and with any number it was two or three times a week. The social set and a lot of others chartered certain seats for the full summer and they were religiously in their accustomed places.

The Monday night Rorick's audience became so notoriously critical and "show-wise" that seasoned performers of later years declared them many times tougher than a Broadway opening." (Elmira *Sunday Telegram,* September 16, 1923)

The first use of Rorick's Glen was for lumbering coming into the possession of the family whose name it was to bear in 1848. Sylvester Augustus Rorick was twelve at the time. At age seventy-five, in 1911, he recalled "dangerous wild animals roamed over the same spots where the gentle little burros now carry thousands of pleasure seekers in perfect safety." The property was sold to Lewis Johnson and his wife in 1893.

In 1899, the Elmira, Water, Light and Railroad Company acquired the glen, with visions of increasing rail (street car/trolley) travel by opening a park on the site of Rorick's farmhouse, "a spot rich in Indian lore and abounding in unusual natural beauty." In 1900, the city's railroads (street car/trolley) were fused into the "Water-Light" but it was the birth year of the Rorick's Glen Park Association which was absorbed into the City Railroad Department and thereby into the company.

Rorick's Glen park opened to the public on "Decoration Day" at the end of May 1900, with the first theatre production on June 18, 1900. Admission to the park was free to patrons of the railroad, and six hundred

Two friends enjoing the sunshine at Rorick's Glen circa 1915. Woman on left is Frieda Janowski. Courtesy Diane Janowski.

seats in the fifteen-hundred seat theater were free, reserved seats cost ten and fifteen cents. To handle the traffic, the company ran trains of three cars with two extra trains running as a section of a regular route. Automobiles, carriages and bicycles were not allowed on the grounds. An attendant cared for all automobiles for park visitors. A loop was constructed with a terminal and large "rustic" waiting room to handle the crowd and the fifty or more street cars needed for after theater traffic.

The property was 125 acres and eventually had twenty-seven buildings. A wooden bridge was put in place which stood on big saw horses to allow people to cross from the north to the south side of the river and the park. Every time the water got high in the Chemung, a gang of men with trucks were sent down the river—as far as necessary to "bring back the bridge." In 1907, at a cost of $12,000 a steel bridge replaced the original wooden bridge.

Upon crossing the bridge, to the south side of the river, one could see the theatre in the center of the park. The theatre, first proposed by W. Charles Smith, (manager of the Elmira Lyceum Theatre on Lake Street) boasted of having opera chairs with backs and arms and all the conveniences of a modern playhouse. The first theatre burned down the night of June 24, 1904. The show went on that summer as a new theatre was constructed. It was described as a "mammoth rustic opera house." One entered by climbing a series of steps. The lobby was almost like a "great porch" and was decorated with a "magnificent display of scroll saw work." There were baskets of flowers hanging inside and out. The sides opened so the audience could experience the cool night air.

Claude Westbrook, writing for the *Star-Gazette* in 1911, described the many features of the park. He observed that, "noted landscape artists have spent much time in converting the glen into a veritable Garden of Eden." Rorick's homestead was turned into Rorick's Rustic Restaurant. Pathways and small brick bridges to ford streams were spread through the grounds. Eighteen picnic pavilions "for free use" were scattered about the glen. Two of them could seat 100 to 150 people. A special feature of the park was its use of electric lighting. According to Westbrook, "the dazzling array of many colored lights near the river, the numerous stars of light appearing along the many paths and from the picnic pavilions—all these complete an electric display that is not excelled anywhere in the country." There were electric lighted flower beds and a magnificent lighted fountain.

Westbrook also mentioned the, "healthful mirth-provoking amusements." One could frolic on the circle swing and roller coaster, or ride a burro. There was a merry-go-round, an Indian village and a gypsy village where fortunes were told and palms read. In addition, one could ride the "Little Giant Railroad." It "puffed up and down a treacherous roadbed filling the eyes of shouting children with cinders—at five cents a ride." Westbrook noted that "intoxicants are not sold on the grounds...."

For many, the thrill of Rorick's Glen were the productions at the theatre. Mr. and Mrs. Harry Dixie, operators of the Dixie Market Theatre in the original Steele Memorial Library Building, became the managers at the Glen Theatre. According to the Elmira *Sunday Telegram*, June 24, 1944, "In 1901 Daly's Minstrels opened the season... and was replaced by the Manhattan Opera Company, first of its kind at the glen. The company was the beginning of what was to become summer theatrical history in this country, for Rorick's from 1904 to 1916 was known as one of the best summer stock opera companies in the country."

The advent of World War I and the growth of automobile use began the demise of Rorick's Glen. The biggest event in 1918 was the War Chest Minstrels which broke the box office record. But following that success activity slowed until, "the management keenly regrets the necessity of ending the musical comedy season. To meet expenses would necessitate putting a prohibitive price on tickets. To our loyal patrons of many years the management assures best efforts for the future when things shall have righted themselves." They never did.

Rorick's Glen was dark until fire destroyed the second theatre in

1932. For several years, where the theatre stood became a stable and riding academy. The property was for sale for a period of time and it was suggested that the Towns of Southport and Elmira buy it and turn it into a park.

In 1944, five area businessmen, Harold C. Varn, Richard G. Raitt, Verne A. Bovik, James R. Beecher and Atty John E. Sullivan bought ninety-five acres with the intention of turning it over to the Elmira Area Council of Boy Scouts of America as soon as sponsors were secured to underwrite the cost of purchase, improvement and maintenance. The Scouts would eventually take over. By 1970, all that remained of Rorick's Glen Park was the dance hall, which would eventually be removed in a controlled burn.

In 1999, the property became privately owned.

MR. BRYAN WILL ARRIVE HERE AT 8:30 ON SATURDAY EVENING

Waverly, Owego and Binghamton Will Hear the Distinguished Nebraskan En Route to Elmira--Three Big Meetings Planned, With Possibility of Fourth—Hearty Reception Awaits Him.

Star-Gazette (Elmira, New York) · Wed, Oct 21, 1908 · Page 2

Taft vs Bryan in Elmira in 1908

by James Hare

The attention of the nation was focused on Elmira during the last week of October 1908. In that presidential election year both major party candidates were scheduled to appear in the city within one week of each other. The Democratic candidate, William Jennings Bryan, making his third attempt for the presidency, was to appear Saturday evening October 24. His opponent, Republican William Howard Taft, would arrive early the following Saturday, October 31.

The election was taken so seriously that the Elmira Association to Prevent Corrupt Practices at Elections was created. The Reverend S.E. Eastman of the Park Church was president of the organization. According to the October 29 edition of the Elmira Star-Gazette, "$500 will be paid for the first information given which leads to the conviction of any person or persons who buys or offers to buy votes in the election next Tuesday or before that election." The "Democratic" leaning newspaper noted that this was in response to "reports of money being used by the Republicans in this county."

The train bringing Bryan, "The Great Commoner," arrived at the Erie station at 9:20pm. A procession was formed, including the "North Central, Italian and Polish bands," to escort him to Wisner Park for the first of his three scheduled speeches. The Star-Gazette reported that, "great surging throngs of people crowded the streets from early evening until midnight, braving threatening showers and at times almost downpours of rain… It is conservatively estimated that in all no less than 10,000 people were within the hearing of Mr. Bryan's four speeches…." It was noted that 5,000 people attended the Wisner Park address, 2,000 were at the Casino rink, and the Lyceum Theater was filled to capacity with 2,000 people.

The Star-Gazette noted that "thousands were deeply impressed with his voice, manner and logic," while the Republican leaning Daily Ad-

vertiser stated he entertained the crowd "with a typical Bryan speech...." On the way to the Lyceum for his final appearance Bryan's carriage was stopped on Carroll Street by a man shouting, "Mr. Bryan they won't let us in the theater. Won't you talk to us?" In response the candidate gave an impromptu ten minute speech to a crowd as large as the one waiting for him in the theater. When he finally appeared on stage a scream, "like a shrill howl of a hurricane," welcomed him.

At the conclusion of his appearance at the Lyceum, and finishing a day of campaigning which included fifteen speeches, he left Elmira after midnight, returning by train to New York City.

The *Daily Advertiser* covered his visit on page seven the following morning.

Republican presidential nominee William Howard Taft arrived in Elmira a week after Bryan's visit. His train arrived at the Lackawanna station at 2:25am from Buffalo. He laid over in a siding until his appearance at 8:30am later that morning. Six bands marched to the station from different points in the city. Participating bands were: Hager's Band, the Excelsior Band, the North Central, Polish and Italian Bands as well as the Elmira Heights Band. In addition, local factories closed for an hour so their employees would be able to see and hear Taft discuss the issues, according to the *Daily Advertiser*.

The *Daily Advertiser* included a sketch of "Citizen Taft" by Robert Lee Dunn. "He is the most democratic of men. He is a Citizen of the world. No taint of the demagogue in this man... He has always been known as a huge man. Some have likened him to a barn on wheels. Yet with all his bulk he has kept it well distributed as athletes say and every muscle of the one time champion Yale wrestler carries its share of the burden...."

According to published reports a crowd of nearly 4,000 people greeted Taft. A large truck had been placed at the southeastern corner of the station to serve as a platform for the speakers. Taft was scheduled for a 45 minute visit. The bands entertained the supporters until the candidate was escorted to the platform by Congressman J. Sloat Fassett. After being introduced, Taft spoke for only a few minutes as his voice was weak from strain and "every word was uttered with great difficulty."

In his remarks he stated, "I note this is the old county of Governor and Senator David B. Hill and I know that he used to count on it as a Democratic county, but I am glad to know that under the missionary influences of Brother Fassett that this county is being redeemed from Democracy and will roll up a majority for the national ticket and Governor Hughes on Tuesday next." Eventually Taft's voice broke and he said, "I can't control my high C's," and he stopped speaking. Shortly after he left the platform. His train departed about 9:15am.

The evening *Star-Gazette* covered his visit on page twelve.

TAFT WILL SPEAK IN ELMIRA ONLY AT D. L. & W. STATION

The Republican leaders of this county are very much disappointed over the fact that William Taft, Republican candidate for president, will give a speech only from the rear end of his car here Saturday morning. It was expected that Taft would remain over in Elmira long enough to give a speech in Wisner Park, or in case of inclement weather, in the Lyceum.

Information has been received, however, that Taft can't afford the time and that his address here will be a car-end talk of a few minutes.

Taft's train is expected to arrive over the Lackawanna at 8:45 o'clock Saturday morning. He will leave at 9:15 o'clock.

Star-Gazette (Elmira, New York) · Tue, Oct 27, 1908 · Page 12

VICTORY ARCH AND MAIN STREET, ELMIRA, N. Y.

The Victory Arch across North Main Street postcard view.

The Victory Arch at Wisner Park

By Diane Janowski

On March 6, 1919 the Cunard liner *Mauritania* docked at Pier 56 at the foot of West 14th Street in New York City. It brought back from France Elmira's soldiers of Company L 108th Infantry 27th Division. Many civilian Elmirans had gone down to meet the ship. On board a special tugboat that greeted the *Mauritania* in the Atlantic Ocean, they held a banner with the words "Elmira Welcomes You Home."

Not everyone came back. Company L had lost 15 men killed in action, 1 missing, 2 dead in accidents, 1 died from illness. Company L stayed in New York City for its big welcome home parade on March 27, and came home to Elmira the next day.

Back home in Elmira, Mayor Harry Hoffman's crew planned a grand parade and banquet at the Armory. Donations from citizens poured in. The committee decided to build a "semi-permanent" arch over North Main Street at Wisner Park, made of cement over a steel skeleton. One side read "Welcome and Honor Soldiers & Sailors" and the other "Chemung County Honors Her Heroes." It did have electricity so that you could see it at night. According to Elmira's *Star-Gazette* on April 1, it was "constructed in record-breaking time" during a terrible blizzard. It was meant to be temporary – "the span will remain for many months to be used on other occasions."

On March 28, factories, schools, and businesses closed early at 2:30pm to let everyone join the downtown activities. Fire bells and factory whistles blew at 3pm to signal people to get themselves downtown. Suburban trolleys brought hundreds of visitors earlier in the afternoon. Veterans of the Spanish-American War and the Civil War congregated at the Armory. "Handsomely decorated" automobiles provided by the Elmira Automobile Club lined up at City Hall for the mayor and aldermen. Daniel Livens donated his entire fleet of taxicabs for veterans who were unable to march. Many other private cars were also donated.

The special train #3 was to arrive at our Lackawanna station at 4:38pm. According to the *Star-Gazette* article on April 2, "the scene when the train pulled in bearing the Elmira members of Company L was impressive in the extreme." There was no great noise, no cheering or flag-waving. The great crowd was simply there to show how happy it was over the return of its soldier heroes. The crowd yelled the names of the soldiers as they exited the cars. The soldiers quickly mixed into the crowd and it was difficult to get them back into parade mode.

The formation of the parade began at the Lackawanna station (near today's Big Lots store on Lake Street). A platoon of policemen lead the parade, followed by the mayor and the Welcoming Committee. Then

State Armory to Be Ablaze With Flags and Streamers On Night of Great Banquet

Robert W. Hoy Is Having Many Decorations Made Which Will Be Hung by Professi onal Decorator—Streets on Line of March of Milita ry Parade to Be Adorned With Banners—Seatin g Arrangements Completed for A rmory Dinner.

Star-Gazette (Elmira, New York) · Fri, Mar 21, 1919 · Page 19

came Company L, the veterans of other wars, and the Boy Scout Bugle Corps. The veterans and the citizens marched through the streets. Leading the procession were automobiles carrying the mayor, the aldermen, and members of the Welcome Committee. The crowd moved faster than the parade so that they might see the soldiers march under the arch. The soldiers marched in "apparent indifference to the personal greetings of the crowds lining the sidewalks. They were solemn and unemotional. They looked neither to the right nor to the left with few exceptions."

The parade marched down Lake Street to East Water, turned right and proceeded to North Main Street. It turned north and walked under the Victory Arch. The police and Boy Scouts kept the streets clear and the crowds out of the way of the soldiers.

At Main and West Church Streets the parade ended. A silent ceremony honored those Elmirans who had died. The group then made its way to the Armory.

The large procession of men were met at the Armory, filled to its limit with mothers, wives, sweethearts, and sisters and finally broke rank. Companies were assembled in the drill hall for an address by Mayor Hoffman. He started by saying, "Boys, we're glad to see you." After the short address, friends and family of the soldiers rushed into the drill hall from the gallery above. After these festivities, fresh hot doughnuts and coffee were served for everyone at the Salvation Army at 155 Baldwin Street. Then everyone went home to their own receptions and parties. A banquet for the soldiers was held one week later at the Armory.

The city thought about taking the arch down as early as 1922. It lasted about ten more years with annual maintenance estimated at $2,500. The last mention I found of it in 1933 stated it was already gone.

Sources:

Elmira *Star-Gazette* "Shall city's Victory Arch be Razed?" January 18, 1922 Page 15

Elmira *Star-Gazette* "The Victory Arch" March 30, 1969 Page 7

Elmira *Star-Gazette* "Happy Days" March 7, 1919 page 6

Elmira *Star-Gazette* "Hello America! Hello Elmira!" March 7, 1919 page 11

Elmira *Star-Gazette* "Citizens Pay Tribute to Brave Heroes" April 1, 1919 page 7

The first Sullivan's Monument before it collapsed to the ground.

Second Sullivan's Monument very nearly built in downtown Elmira

by Diane Janowski

The first Sullivan's Monument dedication was on the 100th anniversary of the Battle of Newtown on August 29, 1879 on Sullivan Hill on County Route 60. Workmen constructed the lofty stone tower of modest materials with an iron spiral staircase to the top. Back then there was no road to the top of the hill, and only the hardiest of local residents went to see it. It lasted fairly well for a while. Elmira men and boys used the experience of walking the five miles to the monument and back as a right of passage.

In August 1898, the Newtown Battlefield committee rode on horseback to the top of the hill to look at the monument's condition, and to plan on how to fix it. The Elmira *Telegram* said, "Their report has not yet been made public, but it is known that the monument, which was originally constructed of the cheapest kind of materials, is in a most dilapidated condition... The staircase that led to the top of the monument has fallen away and only the iron supports remain, by means of which a dangerous ascent can be made to the top. A large part of the wall has fallen away and altogether the monument is in a most deplorable condition. Furthermore, as the present monument is not on the battlefield, but on a hill overlooking it, the suggestion has been made that the new monument might better be erected in Wisner Park...."

Three years went by, and in November 1901, the committee again discussed plans on how to repair the monument. The Elmira *Gazette* reported that "The original cost of the monument was $3,000 and it is now almost in a state of collapse. It is reported that $600 is needed to properly repair it..." There was considerable discussion [at the meeting] but no definite action was taken.

Sullivan's Monument at Newtown Battlefield Park near Elmira, N. Y.

The second and current Sullivan's Monument at the Newtown Battlefield State Park south of Elmira.

After another three years, in 1904, a letter to the editor of the *Telegram* stated that the monument in Wellsburg

"...is beyond repair and that its location, although on a part of the battleground is not desirable... for the reason that is difficult of approach [the road did not go all the way to the top] and suggested that Elmira may be a better place...Let us have a monument that will not only be a memorial of the battle but also so located that it will be seen and recognized as a grand symbol of the patriotism of the citizens of Elmira and Chemung County. Tear down the cheap [Wisner Park] band stand and place the monument there opposite the statue of Brother Beecher."

Signed - An Old Timer

Finally, the original monument collapsed in a windstorm on August 29, 1911. It was 32-years-old being dedicated exactly to the date.

Earlier that year, New York Senator John Murtaugh and Assemblyman Robert Bush, both of Elmira, put a bill through appropriating money for the repair of the monument and hoped that the funding could be used in its replacement.

Legislature quickly allotted $10,000 to purchase the site and adjoining lands, and replace Sullivan's Monument with a new design. By spring 1912, the Newtown Battlefield committee was ready to begin building.

On May 8, 1912, work began on the 1¼ mile road. The road had to be finished before the big granite blocks for the monument could be brought to the top. "The road will take a gradual slope up the hill in the general shape of a fish hook. The monument will be a big needle [eighty-feet-tall] on a heavy granite base that will set on a big mound."

Several weeks before the dedication, Dr. Henry Flood of Elmira went to Washington DC, and met with President Taft to invite him to the festivities.

By August 3, the road was finished but the granite stones from Barre, Vermont had not yet arrived. The *Star-Gazette* reported "the contractors have everything ready to rush work. They are confident that they will be able to erect the monument quickly once the stone arrives. The derricks on the top of the hill are ready. Two engines will be used to drag the 65-tons of stone up the hill."

By August 5, the stones had still not arrived. A large group of workers anxiously scanned the westbound tracks while waiting at the Lackawanna station in Lowman, New York for train #91 that had the first shipment of stones. Freight agents were positive that the train was *en route* to be there by noon, to be followed by three more shipments on other trains. At 3PM, still no train. "The stone for this monument was cut from the quarries quicker than any other contract job ever let there. The contract was so late it was feared the stone could not get here in time for the dedication," said D.E. Harrington, head contractor. " I will have the monument ready for the dedication if I can keep all the men I want at work. A large group of men is cutting down trees and clearing the park."

Several days later newspapers reported that construction was in full swing. The base was completed and needed ten days to fully set. Then the shaft was built of huge blocks of stone. On August 17, the *Star-Gazette* said that a time capsule in a brass box was placed in the cornerstone containing newspapers, books, and documents. It was to be opened in 100 years in 2012. To my knowledge it has not yet been opened.

The dedication of the new Sullivan's Monument was on August 29, 1912. All Elmira businesses and schools were closed for the occasion. Extra trolley cars were enlisted for the heavy traffic to, and from, Wellsburg, New York. Folks first took a trolley from Lake and Water Streets to lower Maple Avenue, then two ferry boats skirted them across the Chemung River. From there, they hiked more than one mile up the hill.

The intention of the day was to make it Elmira's biggest event since the Civil War doings with military demonstrations, drills, and maneuvers

My Aunt Anna Janowski, third row fifth from left, and my Aunt Frieda Janowski, first row second from left were in attendance on the dedication day.

including a big military parade in Elmira with 3,000 men of the Fourth Brigade. The soldiers planned to camp in the Dunn Field area.

Governors of New York, Pennsylvania, and New Hampshire attended. A banquet was held that night at the Rathbun Hotel. President Taft did not come to Elmira, but sent Major General Leonard Wood as his replacement. Lynde Sullivan of Boston, a descendant of General John Sullivan also attended.

Festivities in Elmira included a military review at the Maple Avenue Driving Park, speeches at the Lyceum Theater, a National Guard party at Rorick's Glen, a Daughters of the Revolution open house at the Federation Building, and a grand parade in downtown Elmira.

Sources:

Elmira *Star-Gazette*, July 13, 1912 page 7 "Dr. Henry Flood Sees President Today"

Montour Falls *Free Press*. August 31, 1911 "Social and Vicinity Happenings"

Elmira *Star-Gazette*,, August 19, 1907. "He won the Battle of Newtown" page 1

Elmira *Telegram*, November 20, 1904

Elmira *Gazette and Free Press*, November 1, 1901 "Sullivan Monument" page 8

Elmira *Telegram*, August 14, 1898. "Sullivan's Monument"

Elmira *Star-Gazette*,, March 21, 1912 page 11 "Brigade Officers at Work"

Elmira *Star-Gazette*,, August 30, 1911 "Let Us Have a New Monument"

Elmira *Star-Gazette*,, March 20, 1912 "Maneuvers Officially Announced Today" page 13

Batavia *Daily News*, August 10, 1912 page 1 "Governor to Attend Elmira Dedication"

Elmira *Star-Gazette*,, May 8, 1912 page 11 "Begin Work on Monument Road"

Auburn *Semi-Weekly Journal*, August 30, 1912 page 1 "Governor Dix Turns Back to Days of Revolution"

Elmira *Star-Gazette*,, August 28, 1912 page eleven all articles

Elmira *Star-Gazette*, August 3, 1912 page 7 "Look For Monument Stones"

Elmira Star-Gazette. August 5, 1912 page 11 "Delayed Monument Stones are Expected Every Hour"

Elmira Star-Gazette. August 17, 1912 page 9 "Puts Records in Die Stone"

The Hilliard Corporation's headquarters on West Fourth Street.

The Hilliard Corporation

By James Hare

On August 9, 1945, Edward A. Mooers, General Manager of The Hilliard Corporation sent a letter to Hilliard employees beginning with, "

Now we know," referring to the oil reclaimers which had been shipped to Oak Ridge, Tennessee. He went on to write, "All we've known until the atomic bomb news "broke" two days ago, was, this was secret project number 1, it was said to be of equal importance post war...over a period of nearly two years we have shipped 134 machines to this plant. We are now working on an order for 16 on which the highest priority, AAA, was "slapped" last week...We can all take some credit for having had a direct part in this revolutionary development. We can definitely share the satisfaction of "helping to win the war."

Hilliard's contribution to "winning the war" went beyond the effort at Oak Ridge. The Elmira *Star-Gazette* reported on February 25, 1945 that, "Oil purifiers, reclaimers and filters being manufactured in large quantities for the Army, Navy, Marine Corps and Maritime Commission in the company's two local factories are prolonging the life of mobile fighting equipment as well as the life of the nation's oil reserves." In addition, clutches were made for naval gun fire control and sub signed detection equipment as well as purifiers for refrigeration units for the South Pacific.

The success of the company at the end of World War II was a far cry from its low point in 1933 when just seven people were employed, with an average employment of ten for the year.

The company was incorporated in 1905 as the Hilliard Clutch and Machinery Company. It was founded by William J. Hilliard, "a skillful machinist and pattern maker with imagination and initiative," according to Ed Mooers. Hilliard was born in 1884 in Alliance, Ohio. From there he moved to Erie, Pennsylvania and Niagara Falls, New York. While in Niagara Falls he invented what became known as the "Hilliard Clutch." After patenting his invention and moving to Elmira around 1900, "he interested a number of Elmira men in investing money in a new company to make his new clutch." They raised $54,000, incorporated, rented an old building at 102 West Fourth Street and began production. The building, still in use today, was built before the Civil War. The second floor once was a dance hall patronized by rolling mill workers and builders of the Erie Railroad. The Irving D. Booth hardware concern and the Barton-Wheadon wholesale grocery also started business in the building.

In his history of the company, *The Hilliard Corporation: Past and Present*, Mooers noted that, "On April 18, 1906, 23-year old Max Erhart (Mr. Hilliard"s brother in law) unlocked the front door and swept the building for the first time. Erhart was Hilliard's first employee." The only product made was the "Hilliard Friction Clutch." The company struggled. For the first seven years 1906-1912, "total sales were $25,914 and total loss was $50,075...." A reorganization did take place in 1908, which brought in new capital and a "rejuvenation." The Elmira *Star-Gazette* reported that change was intended to "extend business and make it one of the biggest and best concerns of its kind in the state."

In 1912, W. J. Hilliard sold all his stock, moved to St. Louis, Missouri and severed all connection with the company. He died in December 1956 at age 72.

Over the years the company experienced ups and downs. In the January 1925, the "shop force consisted of 13 men, each working 50 hours per week. The total payroll was $366.98 averaging $28.22 for each employee." Also in the year the company changed its name to The Hilliard Corporation and started making an oil reclaiming machine. A newcomer to Elmira, Delos Giles rescued the company, which was on the verge of selling out or closing. He was aware that General Electric had developed a machine for reclaiming oil to be made reusable. General Electric wanted to find a company to produce the reclaimer under a royalty arrangement. Hilliard secured the contract, improved the reclaimer and began production of their second product.

In a 1957 article, the Elmira *Star-Gazette* noted that The Hilliard Corporation "would be considered today by most standards as a small and solid organization with a diversity of customers that means steady employment and successful operation...." That remains true today. At the time of the article Hilliard had approximately 150 employees, today, somewhat larger, they employ around 490. Now they have two divisions, the Motion Control Division which produces clutches and brakes, with the second division being "Hilco" which produces filtration products. Arie van den Blink (Chairman and Chief Executive Officer, as well as the grandson of Edward Mooers) claims proudly that their market is worldwide, doing business with over sixty countries. Hilliard has well over thirty patents and he notes that everything they make, they design. Now, instead of two standard products, a clutch and an oil reclaimer, they make "thousands of standard products" which can be customized or, if needed, newly designed.

The Old Wisner Park Bandstand. *Star-Gazette* (Elmira, New York) · Sat, Mar 19, 1927

Traffic Square and a Subterranean Parking Garage

by Diane Janowski

Headline "Wisner Park Square Proposed by Engineer"

With the new Mark Twain hotel opening in 1929, came an idea for progress in downtown Elmira. Although the January 20, 1928 headline clearly said "square" the idea was for what we today call a traffic circle right in the middle of Main Street between both sides of Wisner Park. The idea left the Park Church and First Baptist church with 25-feet of sidewalk and grass on their sides. Diagonal parking spaces were allowed next to the churches. The east and west halves of Wisner Park would be united in a central park inside the traffic square. This traffic square was not a new idea, as it was first proposed in 1881 by David B. Hill, Elmira resident and soon-to-be New York governor. Around 1900, it was again proposed by Frank Tripp of Gannett fame.

The 1928 idea was presented to the churches and their initial reaction was "one of tentative approval…. [especially] if the project is carried completely through and not handled piecemeal."

The altered contour of the park would "not necessitate any change in the location of the Thomas K. Beecher statue on the west or the Exedra Memorial on the east." The sidewalks would be diagonally across the square joining at a "circular plot in the center of the park where a monument might eventually be located." Additional shrubs would add to the attractive appearance of the square.

The project was estimated at around $45,000. The engineer billed the project as "looking north from the site of the [new] hotel would be seen the three magnificent church edifices, and the stately old Langdon residence surrounding the square…. [and from the square could be seen] the lofty spire

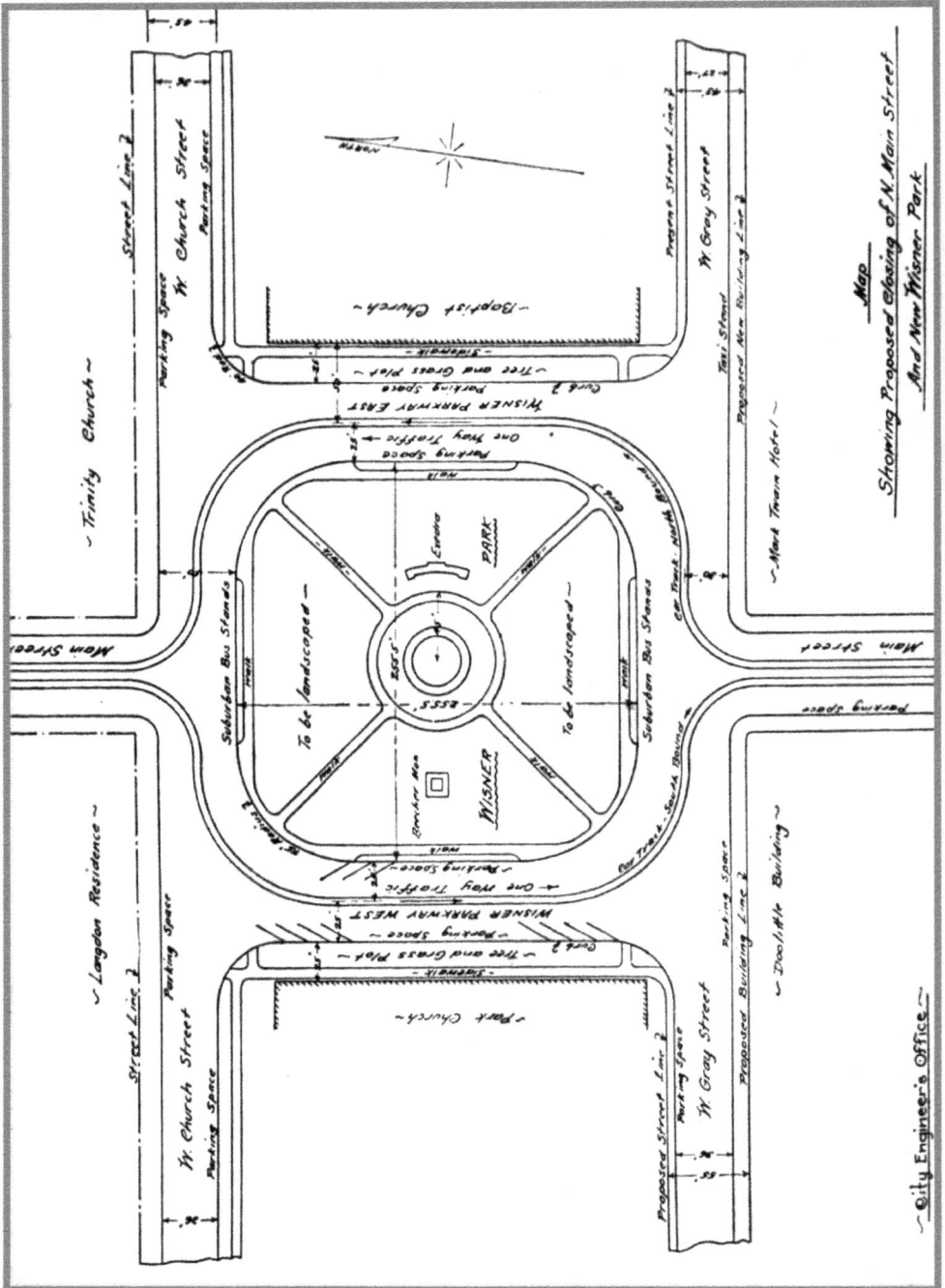

Image from *Star-Gazette* January 20, 1928 page 15

of St. Patrick's church."

Too much public outcry put the kibosh on that idea. The deacons of First Baptist Church eventually said, "We all want a new hotel and we believe it can be had without mutilating Wisner Park." Instead what happened was that Gray Street was widened between College Avenue and Lake Street. This helped ease the traffic congestion in that area.

I found another *Star-Gazette* headline dated January 28, 1959 "Suggest Wisner Park Underground Parking." Now that is the kind of article that catches one's eye. It reported a proposal for "a subterranean multi-level parking garage be built UNDER Wisner Park."

The suggestion came from D. James Shay of the Elmira Fire Department. His idea would have accommodated 500 automobiles on two levels below ground, with continued use of Wisner Park above. Shay got the idea while visiting Detroit earlier in that year. It was in 1959 that the concept of building a parking garage in Elmira first started, as Buffalo was having "astonishing success" with the three it had recently built.

The Elmira Traffic Committee commended Shay for his vision and gave the idea careful consideration. Shay's idea was 212,000 square-feet under Main Street and under both sides of Wisner Park. Entrances and exits would be at Church and Gray Streets with restrooms at both ends.

The idea's only concern was that Wisner Park had originally been a cemetery and there might be legal problems with it.

Neither revolutionary ideas of the traffic circle nor the subterranean parking garage in that location came to pass. Elmira eventually built two above-ground parking garages, and soon we will be getting our traffic circle.

Sources:

Star-Gazette (Elmira, New York) 20 Jan 1928, Friday Page 15

TYPHOID PREVALENT,

Efforts Being Made to Check the Spread of the Disease.

THE BOARD OF HEALTH MEETS

The Board Recommends That All Drinking Water be Boiled—Forty Cases Reported Within Twenty Days—Probably Many Not Reported.

Star-Gazette (Elmira, New York) · Thu, Jan 23, 1896 · Page 5

Typhoid Epidemic

by James Hare

"*Being very thirsty, for I had taken dried beef with my supper, I was about to drink a glass of Elmira city water which by the way was cold, clear and odorless. As I raised the glass I heard a threatening voice say: 'Hold on! Typhoid fever direct from Corning! Drink me at your peril! The doctor and the undertaker will do the rest.' Nevertheless, I drained the cup...Ever since I was a child I have heard, at intervals, the doctor's warning cry, Boil the drinking water! Boil the drinking water, and I have kept right on drinking unboiled water. I deserve my doom...and Corning has not a monopoly of disease-germ either! Even delightful Buffalo—where all good Elmirans are supposed to go when they die, if not before—has intermittent spasm of water boiling.*"

This tongue-in-cheek "letter" to the Elmira *Daily Advertiser* on January 30, 1896 entitled, "Drink the Hemlock" belied the health crisis engulfing the city at that time. Whereas the number of typhoid fever cases reported at the end of 1895: thirteen in September, four in October, eight in November, and five for December apparently were unalarming, between January 3 and January 29 of 1896, there were 87 cases of typhoid fever reported. As a result the city Board of Health had recommended that "all water used for domestic purposes be boiled," including, "all private and public schools."

Dr. William C. Wey, the city's Health Officer, stated that the "epidemic in the city is general." Eventually 439 cases were reported, resulting in 39 deaths. A number of potential causes would be identified, a political battle would be waged over the question of a publicly owned water system and by February of 1897, residents of Elmira would be drinking "filtered water."

THE TYPHOID EPIDEMIC.

Two Deaths at the Hospital Since Yesterday Afternoon.

John Berwick, a Pole, who resided on Washington avenue, died at the Arnot-Ogden hospital last evening of typhoid fever. He had no friends in this city, having arrived in this country but two months ago. He will probably have to be buried by the city.

This morning Rosa Bittner, a German girl, aged twenty-eight years, died at the hospital of typhoid fever.

Frank Walden, who died yesterday morning, had been in the hospital less than twenty-four hours instead of two weeks as stated in this morning's Advertiser.

Several other cases are reported as being very low at the hospital, and it is feared they will not live.

Six new cases of fever have been reported to the board of health since yesterday noon, and three deaths have occurred.

The Elmira water system came into being in 1859, five years before Elmira became a city. The Elmira Water Company was organized that year, reorganized in 1869 being renamed the Elmira Water Works Company headed by General Alexander S. Diven. According to the records, Lewis Snyder, the first customer listed, paid on January 26, 1867 - a flat rate charge of $16.00 per year for water used in "one kitchen and one saloon." The Elmira Improvement Company, which also owned the Elmira Heights Water Company, purchased the stock in 1892 taking over control, but keeping Diven as manager. During this period the water was untreated except for "aeration" at the reservoir.

In response to the crisis in January 1896, the city sent samples of the water to Dr. Chessman, a prominent Brooklyn bacteriologist. In his report, Dr. Chessman believed that "the sewerage from Corning and other towns along the river is largely responsible for the outbreak of the disease, which is increased by the heavy rain and high water in the river during the early part of the month." Dr. A. Cass Jones of the State Board of Health also investigated the causes. He confirmed the sewage threat but indicated other sources of danger. Milk cans, raw vegetables, celery and other "articles for table use" were washed in river water. Ice houses were filled with ice taken from the river. In addition there were barnyards, hog pens, vaults and dead animals impacting the river water.

The health crisis generated anxiety throughout the community. On February 12, the *Gazette* reported, "It seems that during the holidays a party was given in the city for a number of young girls. Since the party, nearly, if not all the girls have had the fever, and three or four of them have died… it has been found that ice cream, either furnished by or made from cream furnished by a milkman who had typhoid fever in his family was served at the party." The milkman retired from his route and an ordinance was passed regarding the cleaning of milk cans.

There were also elements of scandal. Henry Gladke, like many others purchased Buffalo Crystal Water by the case to avoid river water.

He ordered the water from a new druggist, but upon delivery was disturbed by the quality of the water. It turned out the bottled water had been replaced with boiled water from the fountain filled with sediment. According to the druggist, it was a "mistake."

In early March the City Council adopted a resolution which began the process of issuing bonds, "for the construction of a new water works system to be owned by the city." The "Republican" *Daily Advertiser* questioned the city's action. Those questions raised the ire of the "Democratic" *Daily Gazette*, which ran the headline, "A Ring Menacing Elmira" on March 18, claiming the *Advertiser* "seeks to embarrass the officials of the city who are bending every energy to relieve the distress and suffering that has been occasioned by the poisoned water which the Elmira Water Company is selling at an enormous profit to the citizens of Elmira." The article went on to question whether, " J. Sloat Fassett is interested in a ring… seeking control of the present water works system." The next day the *Advertiser* thundered back, "the *Gazette* unintentionally told the truth…when it said a ring was menacing Elmira; that is told almost the truth. This ring has been menacing Elmira for a long time and it's known as the Arnot ring. The ring in its merciless pursuit of gain has not hesitated to take advantage of this unhappy epidemic typhoid fever…in order to jeopardize a property which it is anxious to purchase…."

By May 1896, the *Gazette* had calmed down and stated that the Elmira Water Company is beginning "to get a gait on." It reported that, "it has been definitely decided to put in a filtration plant." The City Board of Health put pressure on the Water Company at their June meeting directing them to "commence construction of a proper filtration plant before July 13th" or face legal action.

By January 1897, a $100,000 filter plant was up and running, with filtered water flowing throughout the city. The Elmira Water Works Company remained responsible for providing the city with water. It would be 1913, that the Elmira Water Board, a public utility, would take over the management of the Elmira water system.

Where Storm-Felled Tree Took Life of Girl

From the *Star-Gazette* June 11, 1946. The uprooted tree that killed valedictorian Barbara Jane Crawford at Elmira Free Academy on Lake Street.

It was the "Storm of the Year"

By Diane Janowski

Inevitably every year has one big storm that is remembered as "the Storm of the Year."

The non-summer of 1816 was called "Eighteen Hundred and Froze to Death." The Tambora volcano erupted on April 10, 1815 on the island of Sumbawa, Indonesia causing a huge amount of dust in the atmosphere that reduced the intensity of sunshine reaching the earth and lowered its surface temperatures for several years. In Elmira, fruit trees bloomed at their normal times in 1816, but buds soon died with the heavy frost. Severe frosts happened in every month of that year in the northeast. Folks wore woolen clothing and mittens even in the summer. It snowed in Elmira in June and July, and crops failed miserably. New York and New England suffered a great agricultural disaster.

On September 20, 1881, came a "Big Wind" according to the Elmira *Advertiser*. "The wind suddenly rose, trees began to bend ominously, houses shook, and terror took possession of everybody. The air was full of the noise of crashing trees and the rattle of loose shingles, skylights, and overturned chimneys. The steeple of the Hedding Church was blown down along with its bell. The cyclone had come from the northwest and swept diagonally through the city."

From the Elmira *Advertiser* April 9, 1928, "damage amounting to hundreds of dollars was caused by the high winds Saturday and Sunday. Cottages along the Chemung River were the principal sufferers. The Phillips' cottage suffered the heaviest loss. The porch facing the river was torn away. The wind picked up the porch, lifting it in a vertical manner. It then sailed over the cottage, gained height, and landed in a field about 50 feet away."

Not a storm, but a day of heat came on July 29, 1929 the hottest day of that year. The temperature recorded at the Madison Avenue gas plant, was 90 degrees at 8 AM, 98 degrees at 12 noon, 102 degrees at 5 PM, and 88 degrees at 12 midnight. The Elmira *Advertiser* said," great discomfort was suffered with the mercury at 88 degrees at midnight.

On January 19, 1936 came the "Blizzard of 1936." A fine light snow left heavy drifts and canceled all American Airlines flights at the Big Flats airport. Trolley snowplows worked for two days straight. On January 22, winds were clocked at 22-miles an hour and it was 4 degrees below zero. The blowing snow on the railroad tracks caused the halt of train travel until the plows came. Some passengers were stranded at the Elmira depot for eleven hours. It was estimated that 10,000 autos were stuck in snowdrifts in upstate New York.

A horrible week began in early June 1946 just days after the May 1946 flood when winds toppled more than 400 trees in Elmira. Three days later on June 11 another windstorm knocked a huge branch of a tree through the top floor window of Elmira Free Academy on Lake Street. A shard of glass instantly killed Barbara Jane Crawford, age 17 and the valedictorian of the class of 1946.

In 1969, Elmira received a blizzard for Christmas with 28 inches of snow. The week of January 22,1978, brought three major snowstorms in less than seven days with accumulations of nearly 30 inches.

In addition, of course many of us remember the Blizzard of 1993. On the weekend of March 14, my diary says, "Blizzard! High winds + 23 inches of snow. Stuck inside Saturday, Sunday, and Monday. The snowplow finally came Monday at lunchtime."

Author's brother Tom Janowski surveys the sidewalk that he just finished shoveling on Esty Street on March 15, 1993. Photo courtesy of the author.

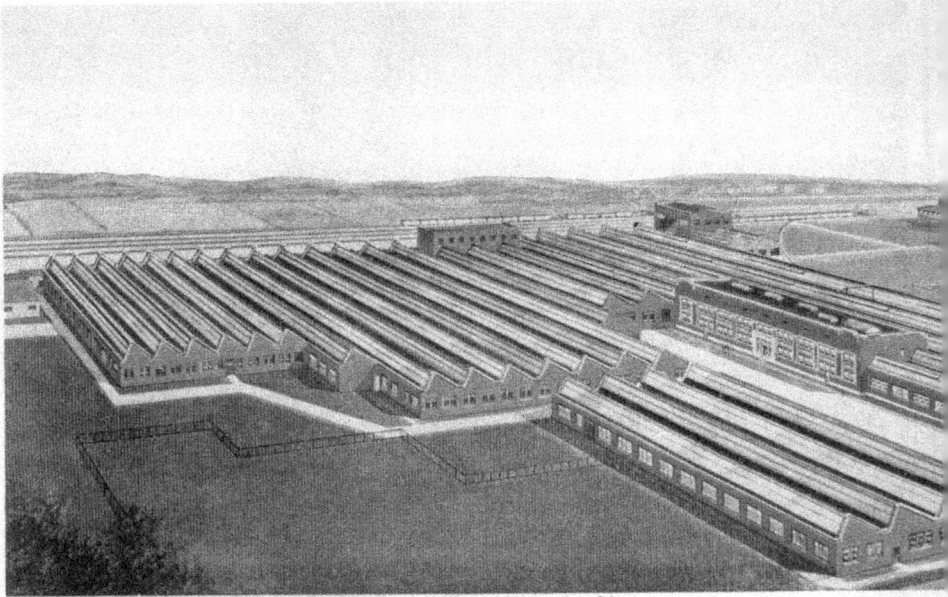

THE WILLYS-MORROW CO. Inc., ELMIRA, N. Y.

Willys-Morrow Company

By James Hare

"Don't decide too quickly; that car has two cylinders and so many may not work satisfactorily." This was advice given by John N. Willys, owner of the Elmira Arms Company, to Fay C. Parsons of Cortland at the New York Automobile Show in 1906. Parsons did purchase the "high powered machine" a "two lunger" and had it shipped to Elmira. Against more advice, he drove it from Elmira to his home in Cortland. The trip took six hours. In a February 13, 1927 article, the Elmira *Sunday Telegram* reported that despite his misgivings at

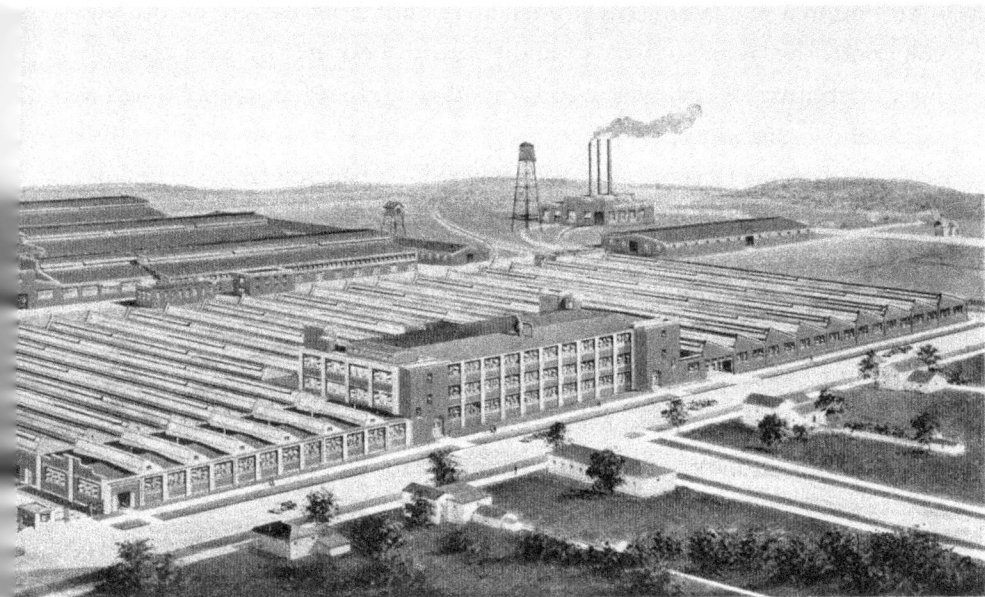

Postcard view of Willys-Morrow plant. Published by Rubin Brothers, Elmira, New York.

that Auto Show, Willys "was sufficiently impressed by the display of budding automobile manufacturers that he closed a deal to represent one of them in Elmira, and thus entered upon a career that was destined to bring him fame and fortune." He was thirty-three at the time, by the age of forty-seven he was worth "forty-seven million dollars."

John North Willys was born in Canandaigua, October 25, 1873. While still in his teens in the days before automobiles, he noticed that the reigns were continually slipping down over the horse's flanks. Demonstrating his "business acumen" he found a metal clip which corrected the problem and did a "flourishing business among drivers and owners of horses and wagons." At age 16 he and a friend purchased a faltering laundry business and turned it around in a year. Using his profits, he bought a bicycle and eventually convinced the manufacturer to allow him to become the "sole agency" for distribution of the bicycle in Canandaigua. In a few years he had a successful business.

He came to Elmira in 1891, where he was involved with the sale of sporting goods. Eventually, he and a group of associates purchased the Elmira Arms Company in 1898. In 1899, Willys first encountered an automobile, owned by Dr. William H. Fisher of Elmira. Willys was smitten.

He met with George Norman Pierce of the Pierce Arrow Company. They made bicycles, for which the Elmira Arms Company was a distributor, but they also made the "Motorette." The motor was 2¾ horsepower. According to Samuel Potter Burrell of the Buffalo Courier Express, it was so low geared that it had to take hills at two or three miles an hour, it had two speeds and no reverse.

Pierce promised Willys the first car turned out from the Buffalo factory which came in 1901. It sold for $900. Willys sold two cars the first year, four the second year and thirty in the third year. Eventually supply would not keep up with demand. Willys formed the American Motors Car Sales Company in 1906 which handled several makes of cars including the product of the Overland Company of Indianapolis. He contracted to sell the company's entire output of 47 cars in 1906. By 1907, he had orders for 500 Overland cars. The factory wanted him to stop taking orders as they were facing bankruptcy. Willys borrowed $7500 from business partners in Elmira and met the Overland payroll.

Willys, using his "sales talent" convinced a group of bankers he had never met to back him in purchasing a plant in Toledo for $285,000. He took charge of the Overland Company (making it the Willys-Overland Company) in 1907, and within two years made a profit of $1,000,000. By 1909, the company manufactured 13,000 cars and 50,000 by 1914. It was during this period that Willys teamed up with his "old friend" Alexander P. Morrow.

Bicycles brought A. P. Morrow to Elmira in 1895 when the Eclipse Bicycle Company moved here from Beaver Falls, Pennsylvania. Morrow was Superintendent of the plant. Morrow—inventor of the Morrow Coaster Brake, left Eclipse in 1905 to establish his own business. In 1907, the Morrow Manufacturing Company was organized in Elmira and capitalized at $25,000. His son, J. Edwin Morrow was a partner and they manufactured parts and supplies for automobiles and bicycles. Originally located on LaFrance Street in 1909, the company moved to South Main Street, built a new plant in 1910 manufacturing machine parts including orders from Glenn Curtiss who was building airplanes in Hammondsport, NY.

Morrow and Willys became friends while Morrow was at Eclipse and Willys was the distributing agent for their bicycles. Willys may have had his first ride in an automobile through his contact with Morrow during an "experimental" trip to Bath with both as passengers. As Willys' business grew, he turned to Morrow to make auto parts. Starting in 1908, the first Willys Overland parts were made in Elmira.

The Morrow Manufacturing Co. had started with one stenographer and twenty-eight mechanics. In 1916, the assets of the company were turned over to the Willys-Morrow Co. By 1919 approximately 6,300 were employed, with an office staff of 275 and a payroll of $6,800,000. County Historian Tom Byrne wrote that the Morrow Plant was "destined to become Elmira's largest industry of the World War I and post-war period." It was reported in 1929 that the plant (located where the Elmira High School is today) occupied 74 acres with 992,000 square feet of floor space. Eight freight cars per day carried the daily output with products valued at $10,000,000 yearly.

According to the newspaper, "at 6 o'clock every morning the long blast of the Willys-Morrow plant whistle informs the 1,600 employees of its day shift that it's time to get up, and housewives all over the city set their clocks at crescendo. An hour later a lesser blast closes the gates on the stragglers. Bouncing from the hills of Chemung Valley, these and other performances of the big siren serve both to subdivide the day for owners of unreliable clocks and to remind them that Elmira has become a power in the motor republic."

A. P. Morrow was a deacon in the First Baptist Church. He stated that he "could not remain true to my ordination vows and continue to be an executive." He resigned as President and General Manager of the company in 1922. John North Willys sold his common stock in the Willys-Overland Company in 1929. In 1930, President Herbert Hoover appointed Willys as the first United States Ambassador to Poland. Both would die in 1935.

Because of economic difficulties with the Overland Company, the Willys-Morrow Plant would close in 1934. The property was purchased by Elmira Industries Inc. for $300,000 in 1935. It would eventually become the home of the Remington Rand in Elmira.

Iszard's
Celebrates

the buying of the Willys-Morrow property by the Elmira Industries Incorporated!

Congratulations Elmira Industries Inc.! Elmira is proud of the valiant effort you have made to bring Courage and Prosperity to our city. We realize what this great step you have taken will mean to us not only this year . . . but in the years to come. We have faith in you....and will continue to show it in every way....by making Elmira the big shopping metropolis for the 2,000 new families that our new industry will bring.

Star-Gazette (Elmira, New York) · Wed, Oct 23, 1935 · Page 32

Elmira Prison camp photograph. Courtesy of the author.

Louis Leon, Captive at the Elmira Prison Camp

By Diane Janowski

L ouis Leon was born in Darmstadt, Germany on November 27, 1841. Louis and his German-born parents, Abraham and Eva Leon, emigrated in 1857 from England to New York's Lower East Side. Shortly after arriving in the United States, Louis and his brother Morris moved to Charlotte, North Carolina. His parents stayed in New York.

During the Civil War, Louis first joined the "Charlotte Grays," Company C of the 1st North Carolina Regiment. This regiment only lasted five months. He then joined 53rd North Carolina Regiment as a private under Captain Henry White. Brother Morris joined the 44th Georgia Regiment.

Louis fought in the Battle of Gettysburg in July 1863, and was taken prisoner at the Battle of the Wilderness in Virginia in May 1864, and was transferred to the Elmira Prison Camp on July 25, 1864.

According to his army service records, Louis was "5 foot 4 inches, with black hair, and dark eyes. He volunteered April 25, 1861 for six months. In April 1862 was conscripted for the War. Was born in Germany but has resided in this country since he was sixteen years of age. His parents and other relatives reside in New York City. Gave himself up voluntarily."

In 1913 at the age of 72, Louis Leon published his *Diary of a Tar Heel Confederate Soldier* as a first hand account of a private. He mentions all of the daily chores at the Elmira Prison Camp, inconveniences, and events – some with humor, some with tragedy. As time went by youthful enthusiasm turned to despair. Some excerpts from his diary include:

July 23, 1864 — *Three hundred more were sent from here to the new prison, which is in Elmira, N.Y., myself with them.*

July 27 — We see the Jersey shore this morning. Our vessel was racing with another. We had too much steam up; the consequence was a fire on board, but we soon had it out. We landed at Jersey City at 12 midnight, and were immediately put in cars, and the officer that promised to send me to my parents refused to do so. We left here at 1, got to Elmira at 8 in the evening.

July 29 — There are at present some 3,000 prisoners here. I like this place better than Point Lookout. We are fenced in by a high fence, in, I judge, a 200-acre lot. There is an observatory outside, and some Yankee is making money, as he charges ten cents for every one that wishes to see the rebels.

September — It is very cold, worse than I have seen it in the South in the dead of winter.

April 1865 — I suppose the end is near, for there is no more hope for the South to gain her independence. On the 10th of this month we were told by an officer that all those who wished to get out of prison by taking the oath of allegiance to the United States could do so in a very few days. There was quite a consultation among the prisoners. On the morning of the 12th we heard that Lee had surrendered on the 9th, and about 400, myself with them, took the cursed oath and were given transportation to wherever we wanted to go. I took mine to New York City to my parents, whom I have not seen since 1858.

On April 12, 1865, after spending eleven months in the Elmira camp, Leon took the oath of allegiance to the United States. He reunited with his parents at 93 Suffolk Street in New York City. In 1872, he married Sarah, and had two sons Clarence and Harry. They moved back to Charlotte, North Carolina where Louis owned a steam laundry, and later a clothing store.

Louis died July 28, 1919, and is buried in the Charlotte Hebrew Cemetery. He was one of Charlotte's thirteen Jewish soldiers.

Louis Leon in 1913. Image from his book *Diary of a Tar Heel Confederate Soldier.*

YOU are cordially invited to the lobby of the ELMIRA BANK & TRUST COMPANY, Main Office, 150 Lake Street, to see an exhibit of

HARDINGE BROTHERS, INC.

1420 COLLEGE AVENUE, ELMIRA, N. Y.

Manufacturers of

High Speed Precision
Lathes — Chucking Machines — Milling Machines —
Second Operation Machines — Collets — Feed Fingers

An established industry in Elmira for the past twenty-two years, Hardinge Brothers, Inc. is a leading manufacturer of the machine tools and accessories which are known as the master tools of industry.

Star-Gazette (Elmira, New York) · Sun, Jul 30, 1950 · Page 10

How Hardinge Incorporated came to Elmira

By James Hare

O n November 28, 1962, Douglas G. Anderson, President of Hardinge Brothers Inc., was presented with the City of Elmira's Distinguished Citizen Award. In his remarks honoring Anderson, Mayor Edward T. Lagonegro brought to the audience's attention, "the long secret smuggling chapter of his past...." The mayor went on to say, "Let's go back to an incident in 1940, when Great Britain's Churchill was pleading, give us the tools, and we'll win the war. Some of the finest tools in the world were made in Elmira by Hardinge Brothers—they still are. But in 1940 tremendous demand developed for metal working machines such as turret lathes. The Hardinge plant hummed day and night to turn out the machines. The precious cargoes were shipped in armed convoys to the beleaguered British. When the crates of machinery arrived in Britain, they were found to have been padded with some high quality wrapping. Hidden in the corners of the Hardinge crates were such wondrous American items as cheese, chocolate, powdered milk, canned meat and other foods, so scarce in England at the time." According to the mayor, such actions exemplified the character of Douglas Anderson, and indeed the company itself.

Douglas G. Anderson and Leigh R. Evans played a primary role in bringing Hardinge Brothers Inc. to Elmira in 1931. But the Hardinge story dates back to 1890, and the relationship of Anderson and Evans to 1915.

Franklin (1867-1945) and Henry (1863-1947) Hardinge were natives of Canada. As young men, they worked as apprentices, with Franklin particularly interested in watchmaking. For a number of years they went their separate ways but reunited in the city of Chicago. On

July 23, 1890, they organized the firm of Hardinge Brothers to manufacture several watchmaker tools which Franklin, at age twenty-two, had invented. Their first factory was an 8 x 8-foot building, but cold weather drove them out. Securing financing from Steven A. Dale, they continued business in a room over a horse stable. The company was renamed the Horological Tool Company, manufacturing fine tools and machinery for watchmakers and jewelers.

In 1895, Dale and Henry Hardinge left the firm and its original name of Hardinge Brothers was restored. Franklin Hardinge held many patents. The "Cataract Line" of bench lathes and attachments would eventually stimulate the growth of the company.

While Franklin Hardinge was building his firm, Leigh R. Evans, a native of Easton, Pennsylvania accepted a position as chief engineer with the Russell Motor Car Co. of Toronto, Canada, in 1911. While there, he designed the first Knight Engine Car to be introduced in Canada and he became associated with Douglas G. Anderson. Anderson was born in Brampton, Ontario and served as a cost accountant at the Russell firm. His interest in the newborn motor companies led to his friendship with Evans.

In 1915, Anderson and Evans moved to Rochester, New York becoming associated with the Morrison Machine Products Company. In 1925, they purchased the company. With a need for more space, they accepted an offer to assist with relocation from the Elmira Association of Commerce on September 1, 1925. On Labor Day of that year, they set up operation in what had been the Westside Car Barn (for trolleys) on upper College Avenue. Continuing to operate under the same name, they manufactured collets and feed fingers (clamping devices used by machinists). They employed fifteen people. In 1927, they purchased the Keybolt Appliance Company of Orchard Park, New York, and relocated it to Elmira.

City's Newest Concern Prepares Factory

Hardinge factory. *Star-Gazette* (Elmira, New York) · Wed, Jul 8, 1931 · Page 12

Morrison Machine Products grew in Elmira and built a new addition to expand their plant. In Chicago, Franklin Hardinge had begun building oil furnaces in 1920, securing several patents. With the onset of the Depression, it seems Hardinge Brothers was troubled by financial concerns. On June 25, 1931, the *Star-Gazette* reported that "Hardinge Brothers Inc. Chicago Manufacturing Company, Will Bring 60 Expert Workmen and Families—Is Controlled By Morrison Machine Company Of Elmira--$100,000 Payroll—Work Starts At Once." The company would be housed in the new addition built by Morrison. It is not clear what the exact deal was but the Hardinge Brothers lathe business, including the company name and the Cataract trademark was moved to Elmira. Franklin Hardinge continued to build oil furnaces in Chicago changing his company's name to Hardinge Manufacturing Company.

The Elmira Association of Commerce had been interested in the purchase and the *Star-Gazette* reported that they were "largely instrumental in bringing it to this city." The Association undertook the sale of stock and aided the project in "various ways."

Morrison's and Hardinge Brothers worked alongside each other under the same management for a number of years. On January 1, 1938, the entire business of collets, feed fingers and form tools manufactured by Morrison Machine Products was incorporated under the name of Hardinge Brothers. By that time, total employment had grown to almost 300 people.

In 1991, it was announced that Hardinge Brothers, Inc. would move its entire operation into its facility on Oakwood Avenue. By that time the company employed nearly one thousand people. In 1995, the name was changed to Hardinge, Inc.

In 1941, in a presentation given on defense work, Douglas Anderson noted: "Until the year 1900 most fitting of mechanical movements was by hand...after 1900 the automobile began to develop a market and the need for higher speed and greater efficiency brought the necessity for

greater accuracy and some measure of interchangeability in the manufacture of parts… Each step up required better machinery capable of
the greater accuracy required. The result is that because of our world
leadership in the manufacture of interchangeable parts in large quantities, American machine tools are recognized as the best in the world."
In 2017, Tom Mitchell, the Director of Elmira Manufacturing Opera-
tions recently pointed out that Hardinge, Inc. "today sells…products in
most of the industrialized countries of the world…our machines and
accessories…are produced by Hardinge subsidiaries around the world."

Stephen A. Swails. Photo courtesy of Wikipedia.

Stephen Atkins Swails, 54th Massachusetts Volunteers

by Diane Janowski

As a historian I often find things while looking for other things. This is one of them.

The Swails family lived at 610 Jay Street in Elmira in the 1850s. They were "free blacks" from Maryland. The father, Peter Swails, and sons, George and Stephen, were boatmen on the Chemung Canal. The mother, Johanna, took care of the younger daughters Mary and Henrietta. The oldest daughter Rachael was already married to John W. Jones in Elmira. The family was listed as mulatto in the Elmira census. Stephen was very light in color and often mistaken for white.

Stephen is listed in the Elmira city directories from 1856 to 1863. In 1863 he answered Frederick Douglass' first call for black citizens to enlist in the Civil War on the Union side. Because of his African heritage, he was not allowed to enlist in New York State, so he joined the newly-formed 54th Regiment of Massachusetts Volunteers, known as the "Swamp Angels," along with 24 other black men from Chemung County. Training was in Boston and was funded mostly by abolitionists.

This regiment was one of the first African-American units and saw extensive service including the Battle of Fort Wagner in Charleston, South Carolina.

Stephen Swails became the company's first black sergeant-major. Stephen was shot twice during the war - first in Florida's Battle of Olustee, and again at Camden, South Carolina.

The 54th Regiment's adventures are chronicled in the 1989 film "Glory," winner of 3 Academy Awards. The film brought a resurgence of recognition of the Regiment's importance in US history.

Stephen fought to keep his rank and subsequent promotion to second lieutenant. Because of his color, his standing was not recognized by the government. After a year of struggling, the US government approved his promotion to second lieutenant, and shortly later to first lieutenant. The company was mustered out of service in August 1865 in Boston. Eight of the twenty-five black men from Chemung County died in the war.

After the war, Stephen Swails settled in South Carolina. He had a complicated private life. In Elmira before the war, he fathered Stephen A. Swails, Jr. This son lived in Elmira in the East Fifth Street area and was a hotelkeeper for many years. He moved to Olean in 1887.

In South Carolina, Stephen Swails, Sr. married and had 3 children. He was a lawyer, a mayor, and eventually a state senator. He was a member of the Electoral College, and editor of the Williamsburg (VA) Republican newspaper.

According to Wikipedia, Swails still has plenty of descendants in Toronto, upstate New York, Atlanta, and Philadelphia. Swails died in 1900 in Charleston, South Carolina.

In 2006, an amateur historian in Kingtree, South Carolina found an abandoned trunk with Swails' personal belongings. A historic marker in Kingtree now notes the spot where Swails' house once stood.

Sources:
http://www.npr.org/templates/story/story.php?storyId=6417951
Elmira City Directories

Monument to the 54th Regiment.
United States National Park Service - http://www.cr.nps.gov/
Photograph of Robert Gould Shaw Memorial, by Augustus Saint-Gaudens
(1848 - 1907)

Ulysses S. Grant. This image from the United States Library of Congress's Prints and Photographs division under the digital ID cwpbh.0389

Elmira Mourns the Death of Ulysses S. Grant

By James Hare

"Mark Twain got the news by telegraph within an hour or two. In a memorandum jotted down the same morning, he recalled his last visit to the general. "I then believed," he said, "he would live several months. He was still adding little perfecting details to his book…. He was through a few days later. Since then the lack of any strong interest to employ his mind has enabled the tedious weariness to kill him. I think his book kept him alive several months. He was a very great man and superlatively good." (*The Captain Departs* by Thomas M. Pitkin) Mark Twain refers to Grant's memoirs which his company, Webster and Company were to publish.

Ulysses S. Grant died on July 23, 1885 after a courageous struggle with cancer. In Elmira, the tolling of the fire bell was the first announcement of the news. Grant's passing, though profoundly mourned, was not a surprise. Newspapers had been regularly, if not daily, covering his efforts to complete his memoirs before he passed. On the day he died, but before news reached the city, the Elmira *Advertiser* headline was, "The End Is Near." The following day it read, "Grant Is Dead."

Many expected the general to pass before he did. In June, Grant attempted to lift the spirits of his family when he wrote, "You ought to feel happy under any circumstances. My expected death called forth expressions of the sincerest kindness from all the people of all the sections of the country. The Confederate soldier vied with the Union soldier in sounding my praise. The Protestant, the Catholic and the Jew appointed days for universal prayer in my behalf… All societies passed resolutions of sympathy for me and petition that I might recover. It looks as if my sickness has had something to do to bring about harmony between the sections... Apparently I have accomplished more while apparently dying that it falls to the lot of most men to be able to do."(*Grant's Final Victory* by Charles Bracelen Flood).

When the time came, Elmirans paid their respects. A Grant memorial service was held on the evening of July 26, 1885 at the First Methodist Church. According to the Elmira *Advertiser*, "as the evening service has been discontinued in many of the churches for the heated season, the audience which filled every seat was quite representative." The organ was draped in black and there was a portrait of General Grant surrounded with laurel leaves. The paper noted that, "the singing by the chorus was appropriate and of unusual excellence." The Rev. O. A. Houghton of the Hedding Methodist Episcopal Church gave the address. Although he had little time to prepare, it was reported that it was "well conceived...and the large audience listened attentively and were well instructed."

The "proper" observance in Elmira of Grant's passing was held on August 8,the day of his funeral in New York City, at Hoffman (Grove) Park. The event was organized by the Baldwin and Fitch posts of the Grand Army of the Republic (GAR). The general committee placed much responsibility on the finance committee for insuring a successful outcome. The *Advertiser* stated that the committee "believe and trust that a respect for the memory of the illustrious dead and also a feeling of local pride will induce the men appointed on the finance committee to make special efforts to secure ample funds to enable those having these memorial services in charge to make the occasion a fitting tribute to the memory of the great chieftain whose death is mourned." It was the plan to show that Elmira was in no sense, "lacking in patriotism or homage for the revered dead."

A large crowd was anticipated and it was determined that lunch should be provided. The committee would furnish, "coffee, hard tack and pork and beans... the patriotic ladies of Elmira would contribute biscuits, cakes, and other goods." It was also decided that music, "both vocal and instrumental" would be made a special feature of the day.

The *Morning Telegram* on August 9 reported:

> *"Elmira was not behind her sister cities in paying honor to the nation's dead. As the first rays of sun shone above the eastern horizon, a gun, itself a veteran of the late war, lifted up its voice and sent echoes resounding among the Chemung hills. It was joined by the bells of the First Presbyterian, First Methodist, First Baptist and Trinity churches led by the hose tower bell and their mingled tones told the people of the city that the hour of parting with the nation's hero had come. The bells tolled the age of the dead general (63), during which thirteen guns were fired and silence again reigned until the hour of noon."*

The paper noted that lunch was sumptuous and that "old soldiers" had large appetites. All stores in Elmira closed between 1 and 6pm. The procession to Hoffman Park, where services were to be held, began on Lake Street beginning at 2pm. Chief Levi Little and a platoon of Elmira policemen led the marchers. Prominently featured was the funeral car, which was 18-feet long and 12- feet high. It was drawn by six black horses, each led by a groom. Three stages rose, one above the other. Upon the third stage rested a coffin, heavily draped in black.

It took an hour to reach the park where a crowd of at least 8,000 people were gathered. (One paper reported crowd estimates at 15,000). Three hundred singers were on the stage. The program got underway with a "dirge" and "divine blessing," "remarks", the chorus and audience singing the hymn, "How Gentle God Commands," "scripture", "a fervent prayer offered by Chaplain Thomas K. Beecher," another hymn. The address was shared by military veterans, Colonel A. E. Baxter and Major H. H. Rockwell. The selection of speakers stirred some controversy because they were not "civilians" and represented both political parties. The *Morning Telegram* responded,

"*They are the representatives of the American people. Both were soldiers, but are now civilians. Through them soldiers and civilians, Democrat and Republican, all patriotic citizens paid their tribute of praise to General Grant. The committee acted wisely as events have proved.*"

In a snide follow up to the memorial service, The *Sunday Morning Tidings* on August 16, 1885 reported in "Left Over Funeral Notes:"

"*The man heavily enriched by Grant's death is Mark Twain. He is the principal in the firm Webster and Co., the publisher of Grant's biography (memoirs). He has already received orders from the army of canvassers of three hundred thousand, and he expects to finally sell a million here and in Europe. The retail price is $5.00, the share to the agents and middlemen $2.00, the royalty to the Grant family 75 cents, the cost of manufacturing and delivery $1.50 leaving 75 cents clear to Twain and his partner. The shrewd humorist had to risk his entire fortune in the enterprise but he pluckily refused to shirk the chance of loss by dividing possible profits and the net result to him and his partner will be a quarter to a third of a million dollars. Mark was a very solemn and decorous attendant at the funeral.*"

Photograph by H. P. McIntosh, circa 1860. *View of people in a stagecoach.* Newburyport, Mass. Wikipedia

The Owego, Elmira, & Bath Stage Coach

by Diane Janowski

Almost two hundred years ago in Elmira, New York there was an inn at 206 Baldwin Street that was a stagecoach stop. In 1820, the "Owego, Elmira, and Bath Stage Coach Company" provided transportation services much like today's bus lines.

In 1819, the Elmira inn was the "hotel stopover" for the O. E. & B. stage. The O. E. & B. was part of a larger system of travel through the northeast. It was a 76-mile piece of a traveler's puzzle that stretched from the northeast states to New York City to Angelica, New York in the "west" with connections north and south along the way. New York City to Angelica via the O E & B line was 316 miles and took about 5 days.

Getting to Elmira was a rough trip though. On Tuesdays and Saturdays, a west-bound stage coach loaded with passengers and mail left Owego, New York at 6AM, stopped for lunch in Athens, Pennsylvania and arrived in Elmira at 6PM just in time for dinner. This was the evening stopover. The Elmira inn does not have a recorded name but served meals and gave lodging to those in need. The next morning travelers awoke early, ate a hearty breakfast then got back on the coach at 6AM, stopped for a lunch in Painted Post, New York, and arrived in downtown Bath, New York at 6PM. Not bad for a 36-hour trip - and only 76 miles.

Going the other way, eastbound travelers left Bath at 4AM on Tuesdays and Saturdays, arrived in Elmira at 6PM. I can't explain the extra two hours when traveling east. The next morning the stage left Elmira at 4AM and arrived in Owego at 6PM. There's another extra two hours that I can't explain - must be a time difference or else they spent more time eating lunch.

The Elmira inn was made of red brick and was a beautiful example of Colonial architecture. At some time in the late nineteenth century an extension to the rear, known as the "Mozart Bungalow," was added to accommodate visiting actors and actresses of the nearby Mozart Theatre. Apparently, many hotels at the time barred thespians as boarders.

The building was razed around 1940. The site today is the New York Beauty and Barber Academy.

From the Owego *Gazette*, January 24, 1826

Owego Elmira & Bath
Mail Stage (Twice A Week)

This line will commence running twice a week, after the 1st of April next, --Days of starting and arrival as follows:

- Leave Owego on Tuesdays & Saturdays, at 6 am & breakfasting at Athens, arrive at Elmira at 6 pm.
- Leave Elmira on Wednesdays and Sundays, at 4 am and breakfasting at Painted Post, arrive at Bath at 6 pm.

RETURNING
- Leave Bath on Tuesdays & Saturdays, at 4 am and breakfasting at Painted Post, arrive at Elmira at 6 pm.
- Leave Elmira on Wednesdays and Sundays at 4 am and breakfasting at Athens, arrive at Owego at 6 pm.

This line of stages intersects the Newburgh and Canandaigua line at Owego --the Southern line, at Tioga Point--and the Geneva line at Bath----at which latter place it also intersects a line leading directly to Angelica, situated about 30 miles from Olean, one of the places of embarkation on the Allegany river, and about 18 miles from Oil Creek, the nearest place of embarkation, and which empties into the Allegany

584 From Owego (513) by Candor, Willseyville,
South Danby, Danby, Ithaca, Jacksonville, Trumans-
burg, Covert, Farmer, Lodi, Ovid, Romulus, Varick and
West Fayette to Geneva, 79 miles and back daily in four
horse post coaches or in railroad cars to Ithaca
    Leave Owego every day at 4 a m, and in winter at 2
p m the preceding day, arrive at Geneva same day by
9 p m
    Leave Geneva every day at 4 a m, arrive at Owego
same day by 9 p m, and in winter next day by 12 m
585 From Owego by Pipe Creek, Smithsboro, Bar-
ton, Milltown Pa, Athens, Factoryville, N. Y ,Chemung,
Baldwin, Elmira, Big Falls, East Painted Post, Painted
Post, Erwin, Campbellton and Mud Creek to Bath, 79
miles and back daily in four horse post coaches
    Leave Owego every day at 1 a m, and in winter the
preceding day at 2 p m, arrive at Bath same day by 6
p m
    Leave Bath every day at 5 a m, arrive at Owego same
day by 6 p m. and in winter next day by 12 m
586 From Owego by Flemingsville, Newark Valley,
Berkshire, Richford. Harford and Virgil to Cortlandt
Village, 40 miles and back three times a week in stages
    Leave Owego every Tuesday, Thursday, and Satur-
day at 6 a m, arrive at Cortlandt Village same days by
4 p m, and in winter by 6 p m
    Leave Cortlandt Village every Monday, Wednesday
and Friday at 6 a m, arrive at Owego same days by 4 p
m, and in winter by 6 p m
587 From Owego by Apalachin, Little Meadows, Pa,
Ellerslie, Chovonut and Silver Lake to Harewood, 28
miles and back once a week
    Leave Owego every Thursday at 6 a m, arrive at Hare-
wood same day by 5 p m

An advertisement in the New York *Evening Post* April 5, 1837.

at Olean; at which place boats of any size are always kept ready for travelers, for the purpose of descending the Ohio River.

Persons traveling from New York, or from any of the Eastern States, to the S. W. States, will find this the shortest, cheapest, and most expeditious route. The distance from New York, via Owego, Painted Post and Bath, to Angelica, is 316 miles, which is performed in about 5 days.

Good teams and careful drivers will be kept on the route, and no pains spared to accommodate passengers. The Stage horses are good.

S. B. LEONARD - March 30, 1819

A daily stage (Sunday excepted) operated between Cuba and Rushford. It left Rushford for Cuba at 5:30 a.m. arrived in Cuba for the 8:34 a.m. express west. It left Cuba on arrival of the mail train at 3:24 pm, reached Rushford at 6:45 pm. This stage coach apparently delivered the mail from the Rawson Post Office. Lyndon residents received their mail from the Rawson Post Office. At one time each resident took their turn carrying the mail from Rawson to the Lyndon Post Office. Sometimes it was carried on horseback.

Sources:
Owego *Gazette*, Owego (NY), January 24, 1826

Renovation project proceeds at Holy Trinity Lutheran Church.

Star-Gazette (Elmira, New York) · Fri, Aug 8, 1969 · Main Edition · Page 11

Holy Trinity Lutheran Church

by James Hare

Organized religion had a challenging beginning in the Village of Newtown (Elmira). According to Edward B. Hoffman, in his book on the First Presbyterian Church of Elmira, "the settlers, like the frontier were rough; drunkenness, gambling, wife beating and later horse racing were said to be the chief recreation. In the tiny village (Newtown) were six taverns. Bloody noses were more common than Bibles." Reverend Simeon James recorded in 1805 that, "The Sabbath was desecrated by sports, labor and business…intemperance was almost universal." On December 16, 1792 a Methodist circuit rider preached at Lough's (Howe's) Tavern in the village and recorded in his journal, "Lord give me humility and watchfulness…part of my congregation was drunk."

The "shouting Methodists" were ousted from holding services at the county jail by the Sheriff's wife because they made to much noise. The Episcopalians held their first services in a schoolhouse.

On the eve of Elmira becoming a city, the Village Directory (1863-64) listed 10 churches. By 1925, there were forty-six churches representing all the leading denominations. According to that Directory, "Elmira could properly be called a City of Churches." For the community the "noble edifices" added to the attractiveness and charm of the city; the "full and adequate supply of churches" was a "factor of progress."

It seems every hamlet, village and city has a Church Street and Elmira is no different. It has been reported that the street was named after a surveyor Philip Church in the 1890's. Rachel Dworkin, archivist at the Chemung Valley History Museum, finds no evidence of where the name came from. But we do know that it is a street of "noble edifices" today, though sadly diminishing in number.

On June 21, 2015 the congregation of Holy Trinity Lutheran Church (314 West Church Street) held its final service. They will be merging with the congregation of Bethany Lutheran Church on South Walnut Street.

The Holy Trinity Lutheran Church building is the oldest building in the city continuously used as a church. Its fate is unknown. The closing follows the closing and demolition of the First Presbyterian Church (Elmira's mother church) in 1967 (current site of Elm Chevrolet), the deconsecration of the First Baptist Church (corner of Main and Church Streets) on September 20, 2009 and of Christs' United Methodist Church (corner of Church and Columbia Streets) on June 7, 2010. The Ray of Hope Church now occupies that building.

In 1851, the First Methodist Church, located on Baldwin Street felt a need for a second church as Elmira was growing rapidly. Two lots on the north side of Church Street just east of Columbia Street were purchased for $700. At a cost, not to exceed $5,700 a simple brick structure, in Greek Revival style, with a centered steeple was completed and dedicated on November 10, 1852. On Sunday, September 25, 1881 the *Star-Gazette* reported a "dreadful cyclone" had hit the city toppling the steeple onto the street. As time passed the congregation grew and in 1897 the Methodists at Hedding decided to build a new church next door making "Old Hedding" available. This was the building purchased by the Lutherans for $6,000 in 1901.

Holy Trinity Lutheran Church grew from the efforts of a faithful band of twenty who first met for Sunday school on July 2, 1899 at the residence of Mrs. King on East Eighth Street in Elmira Heights. Worship gatherings in those early days were held in several places including the old Pennsylvania Railroad YMCA, a store on Grand Central Avenue, an Elmira Heights Hotel and the Elmira Industrial School building. The congregation was incorporated in 1901, and found a home. According to the *Daily Advertiser* of July, 20, 1901, "The building formerly known as the Hedding

Church…will be reopened to-morrow by the Holy Trinity English Lutheran Church, by which name it will be known hereafter…."

Over time the new congregation grew. In 1922, a newspaper report noted "the increase in membership has been 1200% and in financial receipts and expenditures 1300%." In 1941 a bequest for a new organ was received. Installation was delayed by the war but the new organ (still in use) was dedicated in November 1944. In 1960 the congregation dedicated a new $140,000 education building.

The appearance of the church changed dramatically in 1969. Former County Historian Tom Byrne reported in the *Star-Gazette* December 21, 1969, "Until a couple of months ago the century-old Holy Trinity structure was less than imposing. But then Welliver Contractors got busy extending the front, enlarging the narthex, placing 24-foot colonial columns to a new cornice, and assembling, at ground level, the louvred belfry… and topped it with a slender fiber glass spire. The tip of the cross is 113-feet above West Church Street" Bryne then wrote, "With the new column, cornice and steeple, the Lutherans have given all Elmira a beautiful Christmas present."

Star-Gazette (Elmira, New York) · Mon, May 11, 1891 · Page 6

Elmira's Slippery Banana Ordinance

By Diane Janowski

I've been doing research on local city ordinances, and I found an especially interesting one in 1899.

Chapter 9 Sec. 15. No person shall throw upon the side walk of any public street or place within the said city, any banana, or other fruit, skin or peel.

This brings up images of the Three Stooges, Charlie Chaplin, and Buster Keaton films. What is the "appeal" of the banana skin? Bananas were prevalent in the south from the 1850s and up. They came on boats and were unloaded in ports. Southern newspapers reported the litter and danger problems of the slippery fruit peels. Gentile folks also complained of the often vulgar exclamations coming from those who sustained injuries.

Now, this seems funny when reading it, but there are two reasons why this law was important to Elmira.

According to the Chemung County Historical Society, bananas were a new fruit in Elmira in the 1880s and 90s. Shipping from warmer climates allowed huge quantities to be brought to the northern states. Prices were low on this fruit - if you bought them in bulk, but they came all at once by the train car load. Local grocers often had a huge surplus of bananas – so many that they sold them right off the sidewalk. Hungry Elmirans bought bananas and walked away. When they finished, the skins were often discarded on the sidewalks.

Like they say, it's all fun and games until someone gets hurt. A notice in the Elmira *Star-Gazette* on September 14, 1893 reads, "Mrs. James Enright of No. 228 Chestnut Street slipped on a banana skin on West Second Street Tuesday, and fell on the sidewalk, breaking her leg.

The Laskaris store at 144 East Water Street with bananas. Photo courtesy of the Chemung County Historical Society.

Mrs. Enright got a lawyer and sued the city for $1,000 - about $30,000 today. Elmira's City attorney James Bacon determined that the banana peel in question had been "thrown or dropped by someone upon the sidewalk. There was no claim…that the city had notice of said banana peel had been dropped upon the sidewalk, or that the same had been there for such a length of time that the city should have had constructive notice thereof."

I am not sure why but at the next city council meeting, Mrs. Enright's situation was reconsidered and she received a settlement of $98.

Mrs. Enright had the misfortune again to venture on sidewalks of Elmira. Five years later she sued the city for $500 on March 11, 1898 for injuries sustained "by stepping through a hole in the sidewalk on the south side of Washington Avenue west of Benton Street (now Grand Central Avenue." Her case went before the city in 1900. She was awarded $100 for settling that claim.

Complaints against Elmira's fruit dealers continued as late as 1916. Their fruit, and the banana skins, orange peels, and peach pits were an attraction for flies. An ordinance for the covering of outdoor sidewalk fruit was suggested in August 1916. I don't know if that law passed.

The Laskaris fruit stand as pictured was started by two of six brothers who immigrated to Elmira from Sparta, Greece in 1888. George and Peter Laskaris opened the stand at 144 East Water Street, and eventually moved to 131 East Water Street. Besides fruit, the store also sold homemade candy and ice cream.

So, in 2018 the old banana skin law seems ludicrous, but still, if I see a banana skin on the ground I avoid it.

Sources:

http://chemungcountyhistoricalsociety.blogspot.com/2016/09/this-story-is-bananas.html
Star-Gazette (Elmira, New York) 14 Sep 1893, Thu Page 5
Star-Gazette (Elmira, New York) 16 Oct 1894, Tue Page 6
Star-Gazette 27 Feb 1895 Wed Page 6
Star-Gazette (Elmira, New York) 24 Aug 1916, Thu Page 6
Star-Gazette (Elmira, New York) 19 Apr 1898, Tue Page 6
https://silentology.wordpress.com/2015/04/01/the-history-of-those-darn-banana-peels/
Star-Gazette (Elmira, New York) 01 Aug 1916, Tue Page 10

READY FOR OPENING—This is a ground level view of new Sears, Roebuck and Co. store which will open Monday morning at 9. The store faces on N. Main St. and extends west along W. Second St. Parking lot takes up most of rest of block bounded by College Ave. and W. Third St.

New Sears store before its grand opening. From the *Star-Gazette* July 27, 1955 · Page 15

The Sears-Roebuck in Elmira

By Diane Janowski

When I can't sleep at night I "walk around our old Sears store." As did everyone in town, my family and I spent many evenings there in the 1960s and 70s. My memories of that store have a lot of smells in them. I come in the door where the new rubber tires are, then past the snack bar with the smell of French fries and hot dogs, and the big mixer of orange drink. Past the case with roasted Spanish peanuts and candies. We could never leave the store without getting a bag of those peanuts for my father. And then coming around the corner to the big space of the ground floor. From there I could go in all directions.

The beginning of the Sears-Roebuck company began as the Sears mail order catalog in 1887. The next year Richard Sears met A.C. Roebuck. Their catalog service did well in small towns especially with farm families. You placed your order by mail and you waited for it to arrive.

The prosperity of the company allowed for its expansion in 1925. Sears' new philosophy in opening stores from coast to coast luckily included Elmira. In 1928 Sears opened its first store in Elmira on the corner of Railroad and East Market streets in the area of today's Clemens Square. It was only a temporary location as a new building was being erected on State Street around the corner in 1929. Thirty-two clerks would be employed at the store. It thrived, of course.

In 1952 came rumblings of a new bigger store. In 1953 Sears bought a big chunk of land at North Main, Second, Third Streets and College Avenue. Demolition of houses in the neighborhood began in June 1953. The new store's construction began in July 1954, with an opening date of August 1955. It would be twice as big as the store on State Street. The parking lot would hold 500 cars with an expectation of 2,000 a day. Departments included an outdoor garden center along the side, an automotive center, and in the basement were appliances, plumbing, heating, hardware, paint and kitchen stuff. Also in the basement was the catalog ordering and pick-up area. The first-floor housed men's and women's wear, shoes, and children's clothes. On the second floor were home furnishings – furniture, rugs, draperies, fabrics, TVs and stereos.

A *Star-Gazette* reporter got an early view of the store. In an article dated July 27 it quoted, "No doubt one of the most popular features of the store will be the electric stairs which connect the basement, first and second floors." He or she got that right.

The new Sears "one-stop home modernizations shop" opened on Monday August 1, 1955. The parking lot was smaller than promised at 358 cars.

On its first day 22,000 visitors came through the doors. The figure may have been low as counters lost track. Actual sales showed it had been closer to 30,000. As was projected the escalator was the most popular feature at the store. "Some children were counted as having used the escalator 50 times in a row." Eight cars were serviced in the automotive department.

The 1972 flood did not treat Sears well. Eyewitness Denny Smith, who was walking on the railroad viaduct taking photographs, saw that the windows facing North Main Street had blown out. Water flowed in, and merchandise floated out.

Our downtown Sears closed in October 1981 and opened at the Arnot Mall. The building was demolished in 1983 after much consideration. Weis Market purchased the property and was up and running in early 1984.

I wish I had some Sears roasted Spanish peanuts right now.

Yes, Spanish peanuts.

Sources:

Star-Gazette (Elmira, New York) 20 Oct 1928, Sat Page 13
Star-Gazette (Elmira, New York) 24 Mar 1953, Tue Page 15
Star-Gazette (Elmira, New York) 21 Jun 1954, Mon Page 11
Star-Gazette (Elmira, New York) 02 Aug 1955, Tue Page 11
Star-Gazette Elmira, New York) 03 Jan 1982, Sun Page 31

About the authors and this book series....

Diane Janowski is the current Elmira City historian. She is also the editor of *New York History Review,* and was formerly the editor of the *Chemung Historical Journal.*

She has written many books about Elmira and Chemung County history, and co-authored the book *Images of America, The Chemung Valley* with Allen C. Smith.

James Hare is a retired teacher of American History and Government from the Elmira City School District. He is also a former mayor and councilman for the City of Elmira.

He co-authored the book *Images of America, Elmira* with former county historian J. Arthur Kieffer.

Hare and Janowski are freelance writers for the Elmira *Star-Gazette.* Since 2014, they each write monthly articles on the history of the city of Elmira, New York. This book is a selection of their articles.

Be sure to look for our other books!

TRUE STORIES
of Elmira, New York

Volumes 1 and 2

By James Hare & Diane Janowski

www.ingramcontent.com/pod-product-compliance
Lightning Source LLC
LaVergne TN
LVHW011245080426
835509LV00005B/634